SOUNDINGS

GENE W. NEWBERRY

WARNER PRESS
Anderson, Indiana

© 1972, Warner Press, Inc.
All Rights Reserved
Library of Congress Catalog Card No. 72-76777
ISBN 0 87162 136 3

For Kay, Jill, Beth

Dearest daughters

PRINTED IN THE UNITED STATES OF AMERICA

CONTENTS

The Dean of the School of Theology of Anderson
College, Anderson, Indiana, Gene W. Newberry, shares
some of the Soundings he has made as he has attempted
to plumb the depths of Christian faith and action.

He ranges from personal and family concerns to
relevant theological themes to the everyday problems
and events of our time.

He writes with a freshness and vigor which is stim-
ulating, coining words where none seem to fit. There is
humor, insight, creative thought, and deep concern.
The challenge of the book is to think in new and honest
ways about some of the issues of life. How about taking
some Soundings?

I BELIEVE
Soundings in Theology

I Believe

I WOULD LIKE to be an affirming and believing person. It is a healthy way to so live. Daniel Poling gives us a clue to his style. He said that as he rolled out of bed each morning, he sat on the edge with his feet on the floor. He waited meditatively for a few moments and then voiced the two-word prayer of anticipation: "I believe." He could say it once or repeat it a few times. He could add the biblical plea, "Help my unbelief" (Mark 9:24). He could be more specific, as the creed, "I believe in God the Father Almighty, Maker of heaven and earth; And in Jesus Christ his only Son, our Lord. . . ." Poling said it was a good start for the day.

Faith is the soul's venture; it is fire in the heart. Its greatest object is God. Do we, each day, affirm God's presence, God's faithfulness? Can we, following Poling, say, "I serve a great God, and he is for me"?

One day some of us, under Bob Reardon's guidance, put about 20 two-word affirmations on the board. We recall them again and again for our encouragement and support. Do any of these touch your experience and need? You may want to prefix each with Poling's, "I believe." I believe God works. Christ redeems. The Spirit comforts. Faith ventures. Hope prevails. Love cares. Life invites. Time heals. Age mellows. Youth dreams. Fear defeats. Sin spoils. Grace provides. Prayer renews. Christians serve. Church builds. Kingdom tarries. Unity permeates. Joy fulfills. Death concludes.

It is awesome and wonderful how much we have going for us when we become affirming people, when we walk by faith and not by sight (2 Cor. 5:7). Mrs. Rose Kennedy, who has lost three sons, was asked what she thought was life's greatest possession. Apparently the questioner thought she would say hope or love. She, who has known great sorrow, said faith.

Faith has great substance. It provides the foundation on which life's meanings may be built. It is the life-style of trusting, confident, convictional people. I believe!

What Does God Do All Day?

AT THE FORD of the Jabbok River Jacob pinned the angel down (Gen. 32:22-32). Now that is more than *most* of us can do with angels, and it is more than *any* of us can do with God. Note the God we cannot control.

The beginning of constructive theology is the affirmation that the initiative is totally with God. When St. Paul spoke of the new creation, he said, "All this is from God" (2 Cor. 5:18a). God is the doer, the giver, the worker, the caller, the sender.

How do I know all this about God? Frankly, it is not by logic and reason alone, though these may tell much about a universe of design, order, and purpose. The "faith factor" comes first. Our faith always is outrunning our reason. First we are believing in God from the bottom of our heart and then from the top of our mind.

Faith in God is not a kind of teeth-gritting, fist-clinching animal energy. Rather it is the relationship of trust we sustain with God. It is the putting of our whole existence under his authority. It is our affirming of his faithfulness.

"What does God do all day?" is our question. What is he up to in our time? Cautiously and helpfully many have witnessed to their understanding of how the Father God works. First, they assure us that his creative activity is not in the past only, but also in the present. Our Lord says, "My Father is working still, and I am working" (John

7

5:17). Yes, read creation in the present tense. And respond to God's call to be his fellow worker (1 Cor. 3:9a).

Second, we affirm that God can be trusted. The good shepherd does not leave his sheep to the terrors of the night. God is not in the business of humiliating and defeating man. Who can say this in the presence of the world's sorrow and pain? Faith can: "In everything God works for good with those who love him" (Rom. 8:28).

Third, we affirm that God wills salvation for man and the world. He was in Christ reconciling the world to himself (2 Cor. 5:19). This gracious act shows the limits to which love will go to bring redemption. Our guilt, our alienation, our meaninglessness will be met and answered.

Fourth, we affirm that God makes us adequate for the crises and challenges of our living. List them: stresses, fears, doubts, temptations, frustration, grief, hostility. Who can travel these stormy seas alone! The eternal God identifies with the human predicament to assist always.

Ask the Christian about God. The critic, the outsider, may feel that faith is a milksop thing, that God is remote and indifferent, that he has given up on his world. I have never met a Christian who thought so. And I do not.

The Evangelical

ONE TITLE which is increasingly worn by those both right and left of center is *Evangelical*. This is a melodious word to hear, and it has a splendid biblical rootage. Its source is the New Testament word *euangelion,* which means gospel or good news. Many of us surely are hoping the word can keep good company and a good reputation. At present, the two best-known religious periodicals in our country, *Christianity Today* and *The Christian Century,* both are attempting to validate its meanings. This puts extreme pressure on the word, and we shall have to see if it endures.

Let us now join the procession and attempt to invest the word with meaning. If I were using the chalkboard, I would draw a big square, writing *evangelical* in the center. The four corners would be labeled as follows:

Corner 1. *Christ is central.* The evangelical should build upon the foundation of our new being in Christ (see 2 Corinthians 5:17). Through repentance and faith the sturdy roots of Christianity are planted. Our theology and Christian vocation can make sense if they begin here.

Corner 2. *The Word is authoritative.* We speak here of God's mighty acts as disclosed to us in Scripture. It is the largest window through which we look to see what God is up to. May it be at once the record of God's search for us and the school for our response to him.

Corner 3. *Witness and mission are mandatory.* Good news is something to tell, namely, that "God was in Christ reconciling the world to himself." The Christian uniquely combines his words and his work, both always bearing witness to Christ in the world.

Corner 4. *Judgment is inevitable.* We know ourselves to be accountable, in history and at its end, for the challenges given us in Christ. Judgment is not cruel and vindictive, but it is the reverse of the coin whose one side is love. Obedience and loyalty are enjoined upon us. Fortunately, God is the judge and the times are in his hands.

Well, there are the four corners of an evangelicalism which I can affirm. Don't be surprised if many neighboring Christians you know are also trying to lay down these stones of meaning. Let us welcome them to the endeavor of authenticating evangelicalism in our time.

Eight Miles from Sin

A COLLEGE in Indiana once noted in its catalog that it was located eight miles from any known form of sin. It would be interesting to know how parents and students read that little bit of information and how impressed they were by it. Apparently the college was saying there were no movies, taverns, or pool halls in their little town.

I would not make fun of this catalog statement, but I would question its depth and insight in appraising the human predicament. Compare it with Jesus' saying, "Every one who is angry with his brother shall be liable to judgment," and "Every one who looks at a woman lustfully has already committed adultery with her in his heart" (Matt. 5:22, 28). Much less than eight miles from sin, it appears that we are not eight inches from it. Our mistake is not seeing that the separate acts of sin spring from the inner attitude of sin which accompanies us everywhere. Paul called it being "sold under sin" (Rom. 7:14).

Let us put the matter plainly. Sin is strictly a religious term, and signifies a wrong relationship with God. Technically it is not *crime* which is a legal term, nor *vice* which is a physical term. As an example of the two, crime and vice, we could point to burning your draft card and gluttony, respectively. This is not to say that they are not immoral and will not get you in trouble with God. They may. The point is that sin is rebellion against God, disobedience to our Creator and Lord. Martin Luther said, "Sin is, essentially, a departure from God." It is refusal of divine love; it is unfaith. What else did Jesus mean when he said the Holy Spirit would "convince the world of sin . . . because they do not believe in me" (John 16:8-9)?

Sin is universal and sin is mysterious—so much so that though man feels it, he is not able to describe it. There are various classifications as voluntary or involuntary, internal or external, personal or social, of omission or commission. There are various words as pride (man's total overestimation of himself), sloth (man's casual treatment of values and deity), worthlessness, estrangement, meaninglessness. Add them all up and they mean sin, and they are not eight miles away.

I feel we will not have a believable doctrine of sin without a high doctrine of Christ. Our knowledge of sin is enclosed in our knowledge of God in Jesus Christ. All other definitions are too much colored by history and culture. Yes, we really understand sin only in the midst of the doctrine of reconciliation.

All That Ain't Horse

THEY TELL the story in Kentucky. A man sat in front of a crossroads store whittling on a block of wood. A visitor inquired what he was doing. He said he was carving a horse. When the visitor inquired about a pattern, he was told by the whittler that he did not have one, that he simply cut off "all that ain't horse."

There are many who would like to do drastic surgery on the church today; they would carve off "all that ain't church." In fact, some massive tools are flailing and whacking away at the institution, the establishment, the system called the church. To many of us it is painful to see this happen. But it had to come. Emil Brunner warned us in 1953 (in the book, *Misunderstanding of the Church*) that the church is primarily the fellowship of the Spirit and not institutional structure. The church in Russia became fat and muscle-bound and her buildings are now museums. We should have been forewarned.

Most of us refuse to be dropouts in this time of the church's testing. But we are critical. Do we not have a right to be, if we love the ship and stay with her? We are in a lover's quarrel with the church. And it is our faith that "the gates of Hades shall not prevail" (Matt. 16:18). However, we better get on with the reforming, for time is running out. We might do a bit of whittling ourselves, whether as to hierarchy, liturgy, creed, or the awesome system of program and property.

The church is the whole people of God on mission for Christ. How shall we set the guidelines for her future?

She must ever be _renewing_. Changed conditions call for changed churches. Can she be dynamic and experimental, mobile and flexible? If she represents the new creation, she must be, for she alone can make Christ current.

She must ever be _relating_. Her members thrive on relationships, on speaking and acting prophetically in the world. They move from Sunday through the other six days to those endless confrontations with need. They both bring the good news and embody it.

She must ever be _reconciling_. Think of the torn and fractured places in our society. Think of the places where people hurt: in business and industry, in government, in health and welfare, in education and communication, their personal lives. The church brings the word of healing, the message of peace.

What about whittling off "all that ain't church"? Well, it is a pretty messy business and we need to do less of it if we are on an authentic mission for Christ. The church really needs loving and serving.

The Baptismal Plunge

I INCREASINGLY have the habit of asking my young pastor friends, How many baptisms have you had this year? Why am I so nosey? Well, it gets us going on a pretty good conversation. It tells me how evangelistic his church has been, and whether he is bringing the new Christians through the first steps of their journey.

The baptismal step is a big one. Let's call it a "plunge." It is the ceremony of identification with the community of faith. It is *so* public, *so* cold, *so* wet, *so* breathtaking. Is it not one of the clinchers for the new experience in Christ? The young Christian is counting the cost and paying the price. His family and friends know his new commitment.

Why have we treated baptism so casually? Perhaps there are two reasons. Baptism is for believers; it follows conversion. We will not practice baptismal regeneration. Again, we did not want to elevate it to a means of grace, a sacrament; it is still an ordinance. However, the ordinance is in some trouble today because of our lack of attention to it or our lack of conviction about it.

We must be convictional about baptism, for Jesus was. He, of course, set the pattern for us as he sought John's baptism at the Jordan. His word to us is that, "He who believes and is baptized will be saved" (Mark 16:16). Among Christ's last words on earth was his command to make disciples, baptizing them (Matt. 28:18-20). Who can treat such injunctions lightly?

Why do we speak of the baptismal plunge? Because that is about the way it looks to those of us who have taken it. It is immersion. St. Paul compares it to death to sin, burial, and resurrection to a new life in the Spirit (Rom. 6:1-4).

Yes, plunge. To be baptized into the body of Christ means to be baptized into the world of Christ. We are plunged into concern and caring, into vocation and action, into involvement and reconciliation, into the lives of all those around us. Yes, plunge.

Baptism is the symbol of total obedience to Christ. It is the entrance to the visible church, the "ordination of the layman," as St. Jerome put it.

Frankly, I am caught up with new hope and joy about

13

this doctrine. I feel I have underrated it. The ideal pastoral approach would be to follow conversion with counsel and prayer for the infilling of the Holy Spirit—and the baptismal plunge the next Sunday. It would make our worship authentic celebration.

A Goal People

ONE OF THE most encouraging things I can say to my fellow Christians in these stressful times is that we are a "goal people." With a more theological ring, call us the "eschatological community," the group which deals with destiny and final things. If we interpret the words of Jesus in this context, we will do well. Everything he said had the note of immediacy and urgency about it.

We can stoop to a lot of sensationalism in this area of our teaching. It is very tempting to pick a current event or a notorious dictator and pin some moot theological meaning to him. Prophecy is a playground for some fundamentalist theologians. They are really scratching their heads on what to say about the Jewish-Arab confrontation in the Middle East. They will do better to pass it.

What we need to do is work out our sense of history. These seem to us like particularly bad times, but they are not the worst this planet has known. God has great patience; he has been working for uncounted millennia to bring man up to dignity and fulfillment. I need to respond better to his call and claim. I must appreciate how crucial is my every decision, for I stand under divine judgment. If the end of history is delayed, as I think it may be, my personal history hangs by a very brittle thread. Noon today, less than an hour away, may be my last opportunity to see the sun at its zenith. The eternal *now* of my salvation both impresses and frightens me (2 Cor. 6:2).

14

A wonderful chapter for Goal People is Matthew 24. Two things are said very clearly about the end of the age and these are enough. The first is a humbling one: No one knows the day and the hour (v. 36). The second is a cautioning one: Watch (v. 42). Be ready (v. 44). If we need counsel on the manner of our waiting, or better the manner of our working, read Matthew 24.

I like to use the analogy of a journey, a pilgrimage. We must not forget the destiny which beckons us on, namely, the vision of God and his perfect will. Nor can we neglect the day-by-day experiences of sight and sound, of fellowship with other pilgrims. The journey itself is worth our attention.

Think of what God provides for the pilgrimage. A road map! Lights for the highway! Power for the journey! And a "Well done" at the end of the way! Is such talk pure sentimentality? That may depend on your age. To me it sounds pretty good. Let me recommend to my youthful friends, who are ready for a trip, that they pause a moment and ponder the matter.

On Making Man Pie-Shaped

WE WERE studying the nature of man. I remember drawing a picture of a pie, cutting it neatly into five pieces and marking them flesh, soul, body, mind, spirit. I even used the Greek words, as St. Paul does. But actually it was a poor lesson, for man cannot be so neatly divided into separate parts. Recall that E. Stanley Jones once nibbled at something like this when he said that man has two sides, the conscious and the unconscious, and that justification redeems the first and sanctification the second. That kind of theology and mathematics won't make it,

15

for man is not so easily divisible. We can't cut man like a pie, whether five pieces or two.

When St. Paul uses the above words he is referring to the total man, but from a different point of view, a different angle. He is saying that man is at one and the same time fleshly, soulish, bodyish, mindish, and spiritual, if we may coin a few words. The doctor and psychiatrist will speak of man as a psychosomatic whole. The theologian is just learning this wisdom. Georgia Harkness made the same point when she said that it is truer to affirm that man *is* a soul than that man *has* a soul.

One goes back to the old Salvation Army theme for a lesson here. The Army used to say that their ministry was the three S's: "Soap, soup, and salvation." That is really ministry to the total person.

A New Testament scholar has said that as much as 75 percent of the recorded ministry of Jesus was devoted to meeting man's physical needs. If this is true, why do some of us have such great hesitation to engage in involvement ministries of various sorts? Have we cut man up into several pieces of pie?

We might as well jump into the hot water of debate on this topic. It is worth our time and attention. It was the biggest single theme of the Evangelism Conference in Minneapolis. Last Sunday a Christian medical doctor from India was sharing her concern for birth control in her country. The most pointed question put to her was, "What does that have to do with Christianity?" She gave a pointed answer: "I believe God's concern is for the total person."

Should one think of all programs of social and political activism and evangelism? I have not heard that claim made and do not make it myself. But I do hear young people asking all the time where a ministry of divine love might take them and what is the full range and life-style of the kingdom of God.

16

BE ANGRY AND SIN NOT
Soundings in Relationships

✓ Be Angry and Sin Not

THE BIBLE is a most honest and heartening book because it tells the truth about human emotions, one of the most obvious of which is anger. Even the best are not spared, for we have those instances where the temper of both Jesus and Paul was aroused.

Paul is most helpful in appraising and using our wrath. He tells the Ephesians, "Be angry, and sin not: let not the sun go down upon your wrath" (4:26). Of course, "mad dog anger" can make us emotionally sick, but righteous anger can move the cause along. Anger is steam and it takes some of it to fill the Christian boiler. Martin Luther said that when he was angry he preached well and he prayed better. William Ellery Channing (American preacher) said that ordinarily he weighed 120 pounds, but that when he was mad he weighed a ton.

We holiness people are surprised at this. The truth of our sanctification is not that anger is eliminated but that it is controlled. The Holy Spirit helps us "ride the wild horses" of our emotions, anger and all the rest. Paul was on target. Don't let the sun go down upon your wrath.

Let's be affirmative about the matter. Anger is God's gift. Like our other feelings it is intended for his service. Furthermore, none of us lacks it in good measure. To deny it is not only sloppy mental hygiene and self-righteousness, but also a denial of an aspect of God's creation. Characters of the Bible would call our sweetened Christianity unmanly.

Individual Christians and churches should make their anger more studied. If we take our commission seriously, we will never want for targets for our wrath. If we merely feel our anger and do not strategize it into our program we are probably ducking our task. So long as we think there is no place for anger in the face of evil, we will continue as "the bland leading the bland."

Is not the goal of the church in our time continuing renewal? Will not anger be a substantive ingredient in it? We will have some vigorous dialogue picking our targets and remembering Paul: "Be angry, and sin not."

Look at the Root System

I HAVE KNOWN for a long time that persons and institutions have a "root system," but I fear I did not appreciate its importance. The lesson came home to me recently as I read Isaiah 51:1-2: "Look to the rock from which you were hewn, and to the quarry from which you were digged. Look to Abraham your father and to Sarah who bore you." Every sensitive Jew who reads that will tremble, for it still reminds him of the covenant and promise, of his heritage and root system. I tremble because I am a spiritual Semite and Abraham and Sarah are a part of my own root system.

Our Sunday school class caught this truth recently (on Mother's Day) when we observed with Paul that the faith of Timothy's mother and grandmother was alive in him also (2 Tim. 1:5). The words surely had great sentimental meaning for young Timothy. Have you and I looked to the rock from which we were hewn? A very few may feel that they have to live down their heritage. But most of us feel so rich in the tradition which has nourished us that it is a great challenge to live up to it and to put new meaning into it.

Think of the root systems which nourish us—three of them at least—the nation, the family, and the church. One tack you can take is to feel so negative about all of these that all you can do is to debunk them. This is a favorite game of the youth cult of our time. Where does one go if he cuts himself off from his roots? That is not freedom, but deprivation.

Those of us who are working in a church-related college have learned the lesson well: Pay attention to your root system; it is very precious. We are in existence to serve the church and our lifeblood is drawn from the church. We look to the rock from which we were hewn and would have it no other way.

I personally feel very fortunate. My national rootage is American and my family rootage is Kentuckian. My parents led me into the church which has helped me beyond my deserving. These are sturdy and rich roots. My gratitude is beyond words.

Needed: Complexifiers

I NEVER THOUGHT I would be making a plea for more "complexifiers" in life, but I am about to do so. I always thought the world belonged to the great simplifiers. When I was ordained, a dear friend enjoined me to "preach the simple gospel." It did not take me long to learn that it was not all that simple. We are still in the teeth of the debate on the personal versus the social gospel. It surely is oversimplification to fracture the one gospel into two.

Note how St. Paul thought of the gospel's complexity: "This is how one should regard us, as servants of Christ and stewards of the mysteries of God" (1 Cor. 4:1). That verse will throw a scare into you if you are tempted to play fast and loose with life's great meanings. And it will caution you against simplistic and quickie answers.

We surely are not talking here about muddleheadedness or longwindedness. And we are not asking that situations be made deliberately difficult or that we circle round and round a problem just to show our erudition.

Let us say that we would like to evaluate an issue, project a program, or hammer out a principle. We had better pay the price of research, good counsel, and disciplined thinking, or we will settle for untruths and half-truths and not do justice to the great themes of life.

Can you think with me of some of the segments of our common life where the complexifier would be our greatest ally? I could wish we had had some before we got into Vietnam. Remember how obvious and simple that was?

We are calling for some trusted complexifiers in such areas as government and politics, church and religion, sex and marriage, business and finance, education, communication, leisure and retirement, relationships and gaps. All of these are intricate and demanding, and if we find a place to stand, we had better give careful attention. We have been hoodwinked and boondoggled long enough.

As a kind of postscript here, it occurs to me that we need complexifiers in our interpretation and application of the Bible. I am well aware that the words can leap out from its pages to inspire us. But depth study is something else. On a recent Saturday over the car radio I heard an unbelievable mishmash of prophecy and preaching. None asked where, when, by whom, and for what purpose the wonderful texts were written. I felt insulted. On that Saturday complexifiers would have been clarifiers.

On Being in the Center

A MAN WHO boasted of trying to stay in the middle of the road was asked how he could be sure he was there. He said it was like walking down a path and feeling the leaves and branches brush you on both sides. His friend replied, "Do you mind my observing that you apparently aren't even in the road, but in a briar patch?"

In spite of the joke, I would like to propose that the center is a creditable place to be, both socially, politically, and religiously. You may attribute this to my age if you like. Recall with me the judgment: "If a person isn't a liberal when he is twenty, he is a coward; if he isn't a conservative when he is fifty, he is a fool."

Let me say quickly that I have great respect for the radical, the prophet, the image breaker. At many points Jesus is the best example I know. Or think of the upsetter, St. Paul, roaming around the Mediterranean world. Our Lord said he came not to send peace, but a sword (Matt. 10:34). Paul with his companions turned things upside down in Thessalonica (Acts 17:6).

There is another side. If we are careful not to overstate the point, we can also see something of the mediating position in Jesus and Paul. "Peace I leave with you; my peace I give to you," said Christ (John 14:27). "Godliness with contentment is great gain," said Paul (1 Tim. 6:6).

The man at the center is the freest man I know, and he has a lot of room to rack around in. It is a wonderful meeting place for ideas, meanings, strategies, experiments —and just plain, sincere, patient people. It is the context where moot points can be compromised, programs refined, enthusiasms enjoined, witness given, hurts healed. "Sounds pretty bland," you say. Maybe so. But I will take it, twenty to one, to the head-knocking sessions dominated by un-

22

charitable, prejudiced, opinionated, coercive, smart aleck, ego-ridden human beings. "Unfair," you say. Only if the man in the center is an irresponsible ninny.

Too often we have thought of the middle as an un-anchored barge, a messy sandpile, shadowy limbo. If my position is tenable, it must have much greater substance than that. We surely do not have to go through life always being *anti* something or other, an off-the-map extremist, having to achieve status by negation. Do you feel the call to something affirmative and constructive, to something with integrity and dignity, where concern and need find their crossing point with commitment and mission? Come to the center. We should find evangelicalism at its best.

Keeperism

UNTIL I HEARD a sermon by Dick Woodsome I assumed that we always should answer Cain's question to the Lord, "Am I my brother's keeper?" (Gen. 4:9) in the affirmative. Now I know better.

This is a delicate matter. If by "keeper" we mean one who has compassion and caring, we surely would espouse the position. However, if "keeper" refers to one who represses or compels we had better avoid it like the plague. Please do not assume too quickly that we are not guilty. Keeperism, of this sort, is one of the most subtle and shameful of human activities. No one of us is wise enough or good enough to engage in it. It is in very bad taste.

Does this mean that we do not create laws and guide-lines for action or that we do not give each other the benefit of counsel? Does it mean that we do not engage in vigorous debate? Surely not! But we had better guard against manipulating and using persons. We are not called to be people-pushers.

Why is keeperism so improper and so out of style? It backfires: no self-respecting person or nation is going to stand still for coercion and violation of integrity. They fight back, as one should expect. It fans the ego and pride of the keeper until he is beguiled by his own God-almightiness, a condition no person can be expected to stand. It places the ultimate competence in the wrong place. The Holy Spirit, not man, is the great convincer (John 16:8).

Where is keeperism improper and out of style? Among nations. Colonialism is the beast here. It is in a death agony among Communist countries, and others, though it is kicking strongly at some places on the planet. Exploitation of people has to go, whether economic, racial, cultural, or political.

Keeperism is dead within churches. That religious group is in trouble which moves its program by a heavyhanded legalism. Not only youth but enlightened adults also will leave. What does such negative goodness have in common with the new creation and freedom promised in Christ?

The mood of keeperism is inadequate in our families. Think of the human gaps surfacing there. When and how do we cut the apron strings? How do we invest that 18-year-old with a sense of integrity and not slavery? We cannot let paternalism become sour in our mouth.

Well, how are we doing with the ancient text on being our brother's keeper? Do you agree that it needs a delicate touch in the twentieth century?

Religion Beyond Caste

WE HAVE HAD over a decade (since the 1954 Supreme Court ruling on school desegregation) of most probing instruction regarding our many caste systems. It has been both painful and rewarding. All of us must be thankful for the new realism and honesty infused into our thinking.

When one talks about caste, he sees quickly the many kinds of "pecking orders" which are possible. Can you see the roosters and hens in the chicken yard? There is intellectual caste, vocational caste, racial caste, cultural caste, and yes, even religious caste.

One of our churchly embarrassments is that we in the Christian faith trail along like a puppy dog at the rear while government, labor, and education try to break us out of our caste systems. The most quoted alibi is that "you cannot legislate morality." The point we have not understood is that legislation is not to make bad people good, but rather to make innocent people safe and free.

Let us state our points again. First, the biblical point, Genesis 1:26: God said, "Let us make man in our image, after our likeness." That is enough divine counsel to break caste. I dare not bemean one imaged after God.

Second, the ethical point: Race prejudice is the most recalcitrant aspect of evil in man. Commitment to caste puts my salvation in jeopardy. My pride is devilish.

Third, the practical point: Caste will disappear only as men of good will work at overcoming our bad history by creating better history. Windows and doors have been opened on the problem, and we surely are concerned and wise enough to enter the doors and engage ourselves in massive remedial strategy. Caste systems are being broken in spite of the church. Will you run with me to catch up?

Please indulge me a private and possibly questionable point. I am in love with Negro music and humor. I would like to pick up again my Negro stories and tell them with the leg-thumping fun which still accompanies the Yiddish, hillbilly (my own heritage), and Scottish yarns. I predict that time will come again in the decade ahead.

25

Youth and Apron Strings

A CHRISTIAN mother had more wisdom than most of us in deciding her high school son's graduation present. Guess what she did. She took one of her aprons and clipped off the two strings. She wrapped the strings in tissue paper and delivered the gift and "lesson" with appropriate box, ribbon, and card.

No doubt the young man received other graduation gifts from his parents, but none would be more appreciated or longer remembered than this one. The lesson was quite obvious on both sides. The son got the point. One can guess the emotions felt by both parties. They may have been laughing on the outside but crying on the inside. But what a victory! We salute the parents who cut the apron strings and, at the appropriate time, say to the fellow or girl, "You are an adult, and you are free."

National Youth Week theme said that we are "Called to Be Human in a Broken World." "Of course," we say, "what else?" Well, to be frank, I know a few monkeys and donkeys. One of the cute cartoons appearing after an early animal space flight showed a chimpanzee reviewing it with the astronauts and, saying, "Now at 93,000 feet you will have an irresistible urge to eat a banana." It is not so cute when the less than human, the beast, or animal, takes some shape in us.

How do we become a real self and most fully human? Which direction will we take when those apron strings are cut? We are talking about realizing our full potential under God. Jesus told us we are worth more than sheep and more than sparrows. The wonderful insights he shared with us weren't for the birds.

The goal of that Youth Week was *being* and *becoming*. "If any one is in Christ, he is a new creation" (2 Cor. 5:17). Yes, we are called to be human, *everything* that the person can become. The call is to grow, to belong, to be responsible and creative, to be a self discovering, fully functioning person.

Got eyes and ears? Use them. Got intelligence? Use it. Got enthusiasm? Fling it out. Got energy? Burn it up. Got love? Give it. Go, man, go!

Want a text for Youth Week? Try Mark 3:14. Jesus "appointed twelve, to be with him, and to be sent out. . . ." The broken world needs a humanity like you.

Something New and Something Old

THE BRIDE may wear for her wedding "something old, something new, something borrowed, something blue." Come to think of it, these also may be the garments the church is wearing. I believe I can go along with all of them except the blue. The color speaks of gloom and low spirits to me and these I would eliminate.

Go with me to a text in Matthew 13:52: "A disciple of the kingdom of heaven is like a householder who can produce from his store both the new and the old" (Phillips).

Can we translate this lesson into meanings for the new year, the second in the decade of the seventies? What of the old and the new can we affirm? We need both.

The Old. I would like to be caught up again in the ancient truth of the priesthood or servanthood of all Christians. The minister works *with* the people, not *for* them. Thus we will lay the base of authentic lay religion of pastor and people together, in an untiring seven-day-a-week Christianity. We will bring the doctrine of diversity of gifts into its own again.

Again, for something old, let me say that I like the ordinances, all three of them. There was a time when I treated them much more casually. I thought they were somewhat mechanical, not to say embarrassing, observances. Now I know better. The ordinances capture in action and symbol what mere words cannot tell about our relationships with Christ, his church, and our brothers.

The New. Since the church is neither creed, liturgy, nor building, but people, is it possible that in the future we may create "churches without walls?" Meeting places, property, institutional machinery would be treated quite casually. A people on mission, an evangelizing community would have priority. Some would feel that this is our thing in our church. Is it possible that a nervy group will try it soon?

Again, for something new, how about cracking open some granite formations? Alongside our formal bylaws we could place some free-floating structures to meet program and relational needs. Task forces, for a short life, could be organized for a special project or concern. Quest groups (8 to 12 persons) could be created for fellowship, sharing, study, worship, service.

Best wishes as we put some of the old and new together, participating in the renewal of God's people.

He Hears a Different Drummer

WE TAKE our text today from Henry Thoreau's "Walden." He was talking about a man "who does not keep pace with his companions." The reason, says Thoreau: "Perhaps it is because he hears a different drummer."

Tone. Cadence. Drumbeat. It would appear that the young, the middle-aged, the old are hearing different sounds. The drummer may have the beat of idealism, of realism, of fatalism, of cynicism. However, we had better not try to identify a particular age with any one of these. It is not that simple.

One humorous appraisal of viewpoint was a survey taken among Navahos in Arizona. Thirty-five percent thought we should get out of Vietnam. Eighty-five percent thought we should get out of *this* country.

Dr. Harry Emerson Fosdick told of his father leaving an order one morning: "Tell Harry to mow the lawn today if he feels like it, and tell him he better feel like it." Many of us could report such limited communication, condescension, and generation gaps. However, we are overlooking one important point. Though there has always been considerable breach between the generations, it is less true today. At least we know we have a communication problem, are griping about really important issues, are debating at a higher level, and are playing the anti-establishment game with unusual sophistication and charitableness.

Back to Thoreau and the drummer. As we listen to the rancorous sounds today, can we not lace them with elevated Christian meanings: freedom, trust, diversity?

First, *freedom*. This is the most human of all qualities and God's noble gift. Since we demand it for ourselves, we would not dare subtract an ounce of it from others. One thing Christ was not, that is coercive. In the ongoing future the drummer may call us to both the freedom of experimentation and dissent.

Next, *trust.* We have in this word a prime ingredient in the new day of relatedness. Are we able to listen to the unfamiliar with respect and appreciation?

Finally, *diversity*. It is clear that the emerging society will demand of the Christian a kind of flexibility and diversity hitherto unknown. As Thoreau prompted us, "The universe is wider than our views of it."

Can those of us who listen to the drummers project a new expertise? The times are very demanding. He who has ears, let him hear.

29

OUR EGO TRIPS
Soundings in Personhood

Our Ego Trips

THE EGOTIST is the person who uses the word "I" too much, the one who indulges in inordinate self-esteem. His problem is pride, which is the first of the so-called seven deadly sins.

The old-fashioned church organ required a young man to pump the instrument by hand. He did well until he became fed up with the organist announcing the numbers, taking the credit, using the pronoun "I" frequently. He leaned over and whispered to the organist, "This is your last number, mister, unless you say 'We.'"

Let's not kid ourselves; all of us are on ego trips. They may be soft trips on which we become defensive, make alibis, find scapegoats. They may be hard trips of arrogant presumption, haughtiness, insolence of will. Think of the ways we wall ourselves off from fellowship and joy.

A depth appraisal of our ego trips will throw much light on the nature of the human predicament. In the Genesis story of the fall, Adam and Eve are persuaded to defy the command of the Lord by a twofold argument. First the word of God is questioned when, contrary to what God has said, the serpent says that if they eat the forbidden fruit, they "will not die" (Gen. 3:5). Secondly, the serpent argues that if they do eat it, "your eyes will be opened, and you will be like God, knowing good from evil" (Gen. 3:5). Theology sees here the basis of sin as unbelief and pride. Man's sin begins when he doubts God's word (unbelief) and culminates in his attempt to make himself like God (pride). Our "God-almightiness" pushes us into ego trips. They are not merely a social nuisance but a universal tragedy.

In our sensitive moments we know about these ego trips and the way they distort our relationships with God and with others. It is a part of human greatness that men know their finitude, their contingency, their dependence. They also know the temptation to reach out for power, prestige, property.

The opposite of pride is faith, the acknowledgment that one's own life is a trust, a fragile gift from God.

Unflappable

MY NUMBER ONE New Year's resolution is to attempt to be unflappable this year. I have been prodded into it by looking at Reinhold Niebuhr's famous epigram (a motto on my office wall): "God grant me *Serenity* to accept the things I cannot change; *Courage* to change the things I can; and *Wisdom* to know the difference."

Looking at it again, I see it is a prayer. If you also have the predilection toward ulcers, you too may want to pray this way this year. Of course, there are some things we had better become wroth about, even furious, but that is another story.

It doesn't take a prophet to announce that next year will be another year of whirlwind change. Fasten your seat belts—there's turbulence ahead! There will be enough in each day's headlines over which to work up a nosebleed. Would you like, with me, to stop reacting so much with your glands and emotions and start reacting with your brains and Christian faith? The unanxious Jesus (see Matt. 6:25) surely can instruct us.

Dale Oldham and James Massey inspired us on this point when they reported on the World Congress on Evangelism in Berlin. The sessions were held almost within sight of the Berlin Wall. Many of the speakers were from the continent and other areas threatened by communism. One would have thought that dire warnings and vigorous counter strategies would have been central on the program. Surprisingly, they were not. The evangelists at Berlin were unflappable.

In the last couple of years many have rushed out to defend God. (His death had been announced.) We Christians probably overreacted on that one. The temptation to cheap sensationalism was strong on both sides. God seems to say, "I don't need defending, thank you! I can take care of myself." As Paul put it, "He who calls you is faithful, and he will do it" (1 Thess. 5:24).

The winds will blow this year—the political, economic, and religious winds. We do not need to be "tossed by the waves and whirled about by every fresh gust of teaching" (Eph. 4:14, NEB). We will be healthier if there are fewer things we feel compelled to fight against. And the Christian ought to be the last one to panic. Christ supplies the adequacy, the poise. He alone can make us unflappable. He says, "Peace I leave with you; my peace I give to you" (John 14:27). Christian, don't lose your cool!

✓ "For God's Sake, Laugh!"

NELVIN VOS recently wrote a book with the above title. It really started the wheels of my mind turning, as it will yours. Vos recalls for us the incident of Abraham and Sarah having a good laugh. If you do not remember why, read Genesis 17:17; 18:12-15, and 21:6. Yes, they laughed, and God must have enjoyed it.

I like to think that the third beatitude ("Blessed are the meek") may have some alternate readings. An amplified statement of it could say, "Blessed are those with a gay heart and gentle disposition, for the whole earth will belong to them."

The job which lies ahead of us is so critical and unremitting that we simply must have a sense of humor. In fact we had better keep laughing all the time. Laughter is both self-critical and self-confident. With it we learn not to take ourselves too seriously. Best of all, it heals us, for it confirms the idea that we are forgiven. We are free to laugh at all the finite world around us and within us only if we have first surrendered to the Infinite. For God's sake, laugh!

I like the yarns Abraham Lincoln and John A. Morrison told, for they not only were wonderfully funny; they also made a telling point.

An old one about force and manipulation came to mind when the passenger trains stopped running through Anderson. A tired salesman got on the night Pullman going from Cincinnati to Chicago. He told the porter he had an early morning appointment in Kokomo, but that he was a heavy sleeper. "Yell, pour water on me, anything, but get me off at Kokomo." The next morning as the train rolled into Chicago the man was still on it. He raged and stormed at the porter and said he would have him fired. The porter's buddy sidled up and said, "I think he's the maddest man I ever saw." The porter said, "If you think he's mad, you should have seen the fellow I put off the train this morning at Kokomo."

Is it possible that humor may be one of the gifts of the spirit? Let us be merry that we may be serious.

At 55

I AM 55 today and rejoicing in it. I wouldn't trade with anybody, particularly youth. Let it sound like sour grapes. And I am well aware that this is coming to the outer edge

35

of middle age. The date provides me the opportunity of writing my own criticism of the Cult of Youth so popular today. However, that would be far too negative for the joy I feel at 55.

I would like to prime the pump for some others about my age and ask how we are making up our mind about doctrines, about issues, about meanings in our day.

One—I have resolved to let God be God. What a relief! How embarrassing are those memories of seizing the sceptre, of usurping the divine competence. They show up in the temptation to straighten someone out, in prideful arrogance and self assertion, in being casual about worship, in being sucked into tempting idolatries. I pray that growingly I may be the creature, the son, humbled before the Father God.

Two—I am giving up on gimmicks and am going for the gospel. I suspect I fell for religious magic, tricks, extravaganzas, simple solutions, more than I knew at the time. Does not the gospel call for unreserved commitment, Christian love in every relationship, deep biblical wisdom, faithfulness, patience, penitence, forgiveness? Given our principalities and powers, we cannot win with gimmicks.

Three—I was converted as a junior high boy. (My soul, it was forty years ago!) God came all the way to me through Christ. My part was to respond, to respond in depth. The thing I have been learning ever since is how to *respond in depth,* given my age, my experience, my needs. Am I willing to abandon myself to God, "lock, stock and adventure"? One reading of the current revival is that many are turning to God at a level they have never dared.

Four—The doctrine which has grown large for me is that of Christian hope. Death is no longer an obscene word. Perhaps it was the victorious home-going of my dad a few years ago which brought me through to new meanings. But hope is also teaching me how to live with a sense of triumph. It gives me the assurance that the future is open. It gives buoyancy and patience for the rigors of the journey and a vision of the prize at the end of the race.

Probably a sensible man should be defensive and cautious at 55. He is pretty vulnerable. Somehow that is not my mood. However, I have no desire to join a youth cult. But I would like to feel there is still some adventure and risk in my spiritual prescription.

✓ 28 Flavors

I HAVE A secret ambition to sample all 28 flavors of Howard Johnson ice cream before I die. My trouble is that I like pistachio so well that I hang up there. However, I revel in the options.

We come to the gate of the New Year, like ancient Janus with the double face, looking both forward and backward. And what we see in both retrospect and prospect is a marvelous range of flavors, aromas, sounds, colors, and experiences. One feels like the boy who fell in the maple syrup barrel: "Oh, for a tongue equal to this occasion!" But actually no tongue is adequate. It will require a sanctified imagination. It will take the brush of the artist, the hand of the musician, the word of the poet, the formula of the scientist, the praise of the priest to fairly tell the marvels of this universe, and the depth of its meanings.

In one way or another I have thought of the spread of "28 flavors" all my life—from a grade school teacher holding up blades of grass ("No two alike," she said), to my nine dissimilar brothers and sisters. Best of all, I see how dynamic and open my concept of the church and her mission must be. "There are varieties of gifts, . . . and varieties of service," says St. Paul (1 Cor. 12:4-5).

Yes, we are confronted with great diversity in the world, and it is the spice of life. How impoverished we would be without contact with the broad assortment of jobs, places, people, challenges, and happenings. Life's wild mixture makes for significant range and richness. Think of how they have come this year and rejoice. Life is never dull to those whose taste buds are sensitive to the 28 flavors.

A couple of levels of diversity impress me. And they both concern the church. Think of her worship. Let's call it celebration of the presence of God. We know there are many ways to engage in it. We may worship alone or with others, quietly or noisily. We may be informal or formal, singing and shouting, or following high liturgy. We may listen to proclamation or share our testimonies.

Second, think of the church's mission. The program may have elaborate strategy and creativity, or scarcely none. The witness may be indoors or outdoors. It may be an assault on principalities and powers or it may be the quiet identification with areas of need. The alternatives for mission are a joy to behold.

I defend the 28 flavors. They are God's rainbow of promise, his spectrum of challenge and fulfillment.

Sandburg's Nasty Word

CARL SANDBURG was asked, in a TV interview what he thought was the most offensive word in the English language. The air fairly crackled with Sandburg's studied reply: "Exclusive." Exclusive, he said, was the worst word because it was pompous, prideful, and affirmed the walls which divide mankind.

If you and I were playing the game with Sandburg, which words in our language raise our hackles most? One of mine would be akin to his: the noun, "independency." Another, in the same vein, is "isolation." What is so bad about them?

First, they say something shocking about *authority*. I will be tempted by some sort of imperialism, even religious. In a pose of omnicompetence, I will appear to others as playing God. Instead of the appropriate role of witnessing, sharing, and inviting, my Christian vocation will look coercive to many.

Second, they say something about my *attitude*. It ought to be responsible and brotherly rather than one of pernicious mistrust and accusation. We are bound with mankind in a solidarity of pilgrimage and need. When can fear of the unfamiliar give way to knowledge and trust? Divisive attitudes are in pretty bad taste when all of us stand naked under God's merciful judgment.

Third, the nasty words say something about my *assignment*. The meaningful gifts of the Spirit were assigned "for the common good" (1 Cor. 12:7). A deeper understanding of that phrase surely would tell me how to relate, whom to serve, and where to build. It would cure me of my obsession with side issues. And it would save me from the fighting fundamentalism which has become nauseous to many evangelicals.

Back again to that unsavory word "independency." Its implications are frightening, either for the person or the group. It says I feel I can go it alone, without participation with and counsel from my brethren. Heaven help me, I cannot.

Does not the theme of the Christian Brotherhood Hour still call us into judgment: "A United Church for a Divided World"? Can I take counsel from Whittier?

> *O brother man, fold to thy heart thy brother;*
> *Where pity dwells, the peace of God is there;*
> *To worship rightly is to love each other,*
> *Each smile a hymn, each kindly deed a prayer.*

Temptation One:
To Presumption

JESUS WAS temptable, and man is. Dogs are not. Temptability is not man's shame, but rather his dignity. Thus the account of our Lord's temptations (Matt. 4:1-12) is both enlightening and heartening. Note that it followed immediately upon his baptism and was a testing of his messianic vocation. What a context, and what a lesson!

The wilderness of Judea discloses the familiar story of confrontation. On the one hand we have the sinister power of evil brooding over man and, on the other, the constant competence of God to call for obedience. Man provides the battlefield where these two forces engage in ceaseless conflict. The conflict is inevitable: in our solitudes the seducer comes.

Why temptations? Are they not integral to our creaturely role? They test the virtues of the just and check the ruinous tendency to pride. They harden and strengthen the man of God and show the greatness grace bestows.

Look at number one. Jesus was hungry. The tempter spoke, "If you are God's Son, order these stones to turn into bread." The first temptation came unexpectedly in the realm of physical need. Those dusty stones looked like the brown bread from a Palestinian oven. The lesson is clear. We must assess carefully life's meaning and know our true hungers and needs. We will be tempted to turn those rough stones into security and comfort. "Man cannot live on bread alone, but on every word that God speaks."

The allurement here is to presumption on God. He really cannot be trusted and is not benevolent, so I will take things into my own hand. The satisfaction of my own needs and ambitions is more important than doing the will of God. When self preservation is at stake, we are tempted to self pity and grumbling. We are fascinated by miracles and their answer to satisfying immediate needs.

The thraldom here is idolatry to the physical. This is the "glittering things" temptation. It is the problem of putting second things first, of valuing material security more than the vision of God. Do you and I know some who extol the gifts of God instead of the giver, and who worship the help instead of the helper, the medicine instead of the physician, the bread instead of the God who cares? Could you and I be guilty of it?

Lesson one asks powerfully if God is dead in our existence. We probe deeply for a valid trust in him. We do it with the help and example of one who said, "Do not be anxious about your life, what you shall eat . . . Is not life more than food?" (Matt. 6:25).

Temptation Two: To Dazzlement

IF WE THINK the first temptation—to satisfy physical needs (turning stones into bread)—is great, we haven't seen anything yet. That one hits us about three times a day; the second comes twenty-four times and more a day. The enemy urged Jesus to throw himself down from the pinnacle of the temple (Matt. 4:5-7). He assured Jesus that he would not be hurt.

Recall that Jesus was just beginning his vocation. The act would be a spectacular demonstration and a convincing sign for the young minister. (Has any young minister not met this one?) Thus our Lord begins the continuous battle with the ego—the temptation to dazzlement.

Note that Jesus has now gone into the city. He is surrounded by competing kinds of pageantry. Here is the colorful temple fanfare, the eager people, the priests, the Pharisees. He is looking out from a high place. Take a guess on what he sees from there, and who sees him.

What was it? The temptation to thrust oneself into peril and compel God to intervene. The temptation to create a crisis and call God's hand. Who has not known this business of trying to back God into a corner? We occassionally do it economically, or spiritually, or theologically. We set our teeth on having our own way and insist that God make us look good in meeting our claims.

Man has an insatiable appetite for "signs." We pester God just as the Pharisees pestered Jesus (Mark 8:11). We want God to "throw a miracle." We call for healings, prophecies, tongues. Jesus "sighed deeply" when these pressures developed. He said no sign would be given.

What is the basic problem posed by temptation two? It is a massive misunderstanding of how to found the Kingdom and what its ingredients are. It is a misappraisal of God's plan and method. We are not free to call in God's power in order to parade it, to *use* it. He will not let us make a carnival and sideshow out of it. Note how substantial, yet delicate, the divine mission is. God is the creator, servant, lover, who cares much about lilies, sparrows, hairs, and little ones.

This latter touches me and my fellow ministers at a very tender spot. We have great love for the temple and holy places. We become masters at clerical and temple games. Let's not kid ourselves. We engage in an embarrassing amount of temple gimmickery and hocus-pocus. Pray the preacher's prayer with me: "O Lord, forgive me the petty vanities that let me forget the author and finisher of my faith, and the grandiose pride which tempts me to play God." Amen.

Temptation 3:
Shining Landscape

LOOK AT Jesus' three temptations with me again to
see how they continually recur. First, the temptation to
self-preservation (turning stones into bread). We are
tempted to work miracles to satisfy immediate needs.
Second, the temptation to public acclamation (throw himself down from the temple). We are tempted to become
a celebrity by giving convincing signs. Third, the temptation to world domination (receive the kingdoms of the
world for falling down to worship the devil). We are
tempted to exercise coercive spiritual and political power.

The temptations followed the ecstasy of our Lord's
baptism. Here he comes to a deep searching of his heart,
a thinking through of his mission. And this is always
lonely business. Recall the forks of the road where we
encounter a formidable opponent, and must choose. The
risks and conflicts are eternally with us. But we have as
great a chance to rise as to fall.

One writer (Helmut Thielicke) has called temptation
three that of the "shining landscape." "Look," says the
tempter, "see those kingdoms!" All this honor and power
will be Israel's and Israel's God's. There is wealth, authority, and glory for you who have had so little.

One has to put himself into the shoes of a vigorous
young Hebrew and think of his people's dreams. The
Jews were a scattered and harrassed people. Roman gar-
risons were in their towns, taxing and oppressing. How
they hungered for kingdoms of peace for themselves and
God's glory! Jesus must have shared this patriotic pas-
sion. Here is the chance to arouse the fighting blood of
Israel. The bait is eminence and glory. The temptation

is to take the road of expediency and compromise. The option is to be spat upon, beaten, burned, crucified.

The question: How does the shining landscape confront us in our vocation? How do we respond to the many urges to prestige and power, to exalt self in one way or another? What about those times when ordinary virtues do not seem enough, and the humble way of the Christian looks very hard?

Let's be honest and realistic. Caesar's sword and the Inquisition will not scourge us. The compromises will be smaller and the temptations subtler. We will rather be tempted to run and hide, to resist engagement and involvement, to take Christ lightly, to forget the demands of charity and justice.

Recall Jesus' strong defense. His mind was glowing with a wisdom from Psalm 91. With it, he was able to speak powerfully, "Begone, Satan!" (Matt. 4:10).

SERVANTS IN THE SEVENTIES

Soundings in Service

Servants in the Seventies

A FEW DAYS ago we celebrated the ordinance of the basin and the towel (John 13:3-17). I have heard some call it the rite of purification, before breaking bread. That interpretation is wide of the mark. Better call it the symbol of the servant people. Our Lord, who identified with the suffering people, our Lord, who identified with the suffering servant of Isaiah, presented an inspiring action sermon, a parable in deeds. He said, "Whoever would be great among you must be your servant" (Matt. 20:26). The disciples got the point: Jesus moved among them as one who served.

As obvious as it is from Scripture, we in the seventies are just catching on to the concept of the servant church. One might say that the pastor is the servant of the servants of God. The greater truth is not that of the ruling hierarchy, but rather that of the serving laity. Unless we become tremendously creative in mission and outreach we may have a "servant problem" in the church. What if a congregation took the pastor seriously when he exhorted them to find a handle of service, and showed up Sunday afternoon, asking, "What did you have in mind?"

I know a church where pastors and people have selected ten areas where concern is expressed and service given. Students on our various college campuses are learning the lesson for life. Over two hundred from Anderson College were engaged last summer in Tri-S: Student Summer Service. They will never be the same; nor will the campus.

We serve God and man. We serve children, youth and adults. We serve saint and sinner. We serve the community and the world.

There is an institutional crisis in Christendom and it is partly due to disengagement from society and the world. Credibility would be restored quickly if we became the servant people. Can we engage the world on its own ground and plant the leaven, salt, light, and bread of the gospel and let them work? If we are looking for the renewal of the church, servantship is the tack to take. It is unassailable.

The Barren Fig Tree

THE ENTRY HALL of the seminary has an impressive piece of metal sculpture: a barren fig tree (Matt. 21:19-20). It carries an appropriate message for faculty and students, namely, that judgment will fall on pretentious but fruitless lives. I shudder before this truth.

There is a very disquieting section in Leviticus (22:20-22) about the quality of the offering we make to God: "Whatsoever hath a blemish, that shall ye not offer: for it shall not be acceptable for you. . . . Blind, or broken, or maimed, or having a wen, or scurvy, or scabbed, ye shall not offer these unto the Lord." The picture here is that of a farmer chasing down a mangy old animal, about to die anyway, to satisfy his vows to God. The word from God through Moses is that second-class, blemished offerings will not be accepted. God requires the best from our head, hands, and heart.

We are talking about the matter of Christian giving. One of the most shocking confessions in all Christendom is that of our flabby stewardship, our casual response to God's total giving. Is our problem that we are hung up on the tithe, or that we are thinking of some scheme to raise money for the church? Surely we do not believe that man himself is responsible for creating time, energy, tal-

ents, lands, or grace itself. None of these really is pos-
sessed by man; rather they are lent. It is our misfortune
and sin to fancy they are given. It is all His; it is all God's.
We relinquish them at death. To learn this may come close
to learning life's biggest lesson.

This is God's strange economy, his means of calling us
into active partnership with himself. It may be compared
to the battery of an automobile which is meant not to
store up power for itself but to give its energy for the
benefit of other parts of the car.

Stewardship, in this elevated sense, is the noblest expression of the Christian ideal and provides the motivation
for significant achievement. It does so by leading the way
to discipline, sacrifice, and service through which one finds
the victorious life. Stewardship is our commitment, the
asking of God to take us back unto himself, all that we
have and that we are. It is all that a man does after he says,
"I believe."

Paul Tournier says that "the supreme gift is the giving
of oneself." It will save us from barrenness. And it will
help us live honorably with Jesus' counsel: "Every one
to whom much is given, of him will much be required"
(Luke 12:48).

"Help, I'm a Layman!"

LAYMEN ARE DISCOVERED, discussed, decorated,
dunned, challenged, canvassed, celebrated, carved, spon-
sored, scolded, solaced, silenced, talked to, prayed for,
wept about. No wonder they shout, "Help, I'm a layman!"

Layman comes from the New Testament word *laos,*
meaning "people," as in 1 Peter 2:9-10. So, laymen are
the whole people of God. All of us, including clergy,
hopefully qualify. In common usage, however, the term
layman is inadequate; it usually means one who does not

practice, or is just an observer. We must always keep doing our homework with this word. The New Testament, of course, is clear at this point; all were called as recruits in Christ's cause. Thus, the ministry of the people of God must be seen as universal and inclusive of all the relationships of our common life. Paul put it pointedly to a New Testament layman in Colossians 4:17: "Say to Archippus, 'See that you fulfill the ministry which you have received in the Lord.' "

Dr. Elton Trueblood has listed the marks of the Christian layman as follows: the reality of Commitment, the acceptance of a Discipline, the bearing of a Witness, the participation in a Ministry, and the sharing of a deep Fellowship. The laity then are not helpers of the clergy so the clergy can do their jobs, but the clergy are the helpers of the whole people of God so the laity can be the church.

The theme for a Laymen's Sunday was "Christ's Ambassadors." Since an ambassador is one who is "sent," the theme is a bit misleading. In the realest sense, laymen do not go on mission; they are already there. We must capitalize much more on this fact, namely, that the laymen are given a presence in the world. More than that, they know the world. They have an inside understanding of opportunities, problems, needs, and dangers. They also control the resources needed for ministry in the world. They have competence, energy, strategies, and funds to make sense out of it. Can we affirm helpfully the truth that lay people, the unordained, are called to this ministry? As Albert Outler puts it, "The clergy can bring the church up to a new frontier, but it is the laity that must effect the crossing and managing the settlement on the lands beyond."

All of us are thrilled in this new day of the emancipation of laymen. So far, however, we have not done much about it. The game has yet to be played and the victory to be won. Every minister must learn how to reply supportingly when he hears the scream, "Help, I'm a layman!"

Playing with
Evangelistic Percentages

MANY CHRISTIANS have a bad conscience because they are not "soul winners." The minister will encourage us to carry a concern for our neighbor and to attempt to win him to Christ. We do not mean to treat the matter casually, but we usually chicken out on any confrontation. Shall we ask why? I can think of two reasons.

First, we lack confidence, skill, and training in soul winning. It may be talked about and enjoined upon us, but we have far too few examples of it being accomplished. We need to treat each other with greater theological honesty and vocational fairness.

Second, and this is a hard saying, soul winning may be mainly a priestly or pastoral assignment—or, at least, reserved for say 5 percent of especially gifted and trained laymen. If I were pastoring a congregation of 100 I would be delighted to have five others join me in bringing men and women to Christ and to Christian baptism. Now that 5 percent is not a magical (or even biblical) number, but to some it is more believable and feasible than throwing the net out to capture 100 percent for personal evangelism. I am tired of hearing the church scolded for its inattention to the evangelistic challenge.

What about the other 95 percent? Again, let's be totally honest, though a bit arbitrary with the figures, for argument's sake. I would like to see another 45 percent committed, zealous, and winsome in their witness for Christ and his church in an untiring, seven-day-a-week Christianity. They have the courage of their convictions, familiarity with the Word of God, knowledge of current issues, competence to relate to others feelingly, always humble and teachable. What an order! But why shouldn't we see more of it if pastor and people are moving under the banner of Christ's love and power?

That leaves 50 percent. They are very precious. They are circling the field with us Sunday after Sunday, seeing if they like the territory. They are nibbling at the gospel to see if it is good. They are listening to and observing the rest of us intently. Some are standing by the door wondering if they should enter. Some have entered, but they would be the first to call themselves babes in Christ. We would throw our arms around them and welcome them in joining us as we become the church we were meant to be.

Having picked these percentages out of the air, I am still wondering about their validity. What do *you* think?

"There Is a Time"—1970s

THE DECADE of the seventies has broken in upon us. At my age, these ten-year blocks seem frightfully important. I wasn't ready for this one. I feel like the porcupine hunter. He said he hunted with a big tub, stalking the animal through the brush and throwing the tub over him. When asked about this method, he said that it gave him something to sit on while he plotted his next move. Here we sit at the gate of the year, and the decade, thinking. But we have more than a porcupine under the tub.

Look at Ecclesiastes 3 for a list of things to think about, a schedule of "seasons" ahead. There are twenty-eight, including "a time to weep, and a time to laugh; a time to love, and a time to hate." It is remarkably comprehensive and up-to-date. It is my guess that we shall face all these times in the decade ahead with new intensity.

How are your optimism and hope for the next ten years? Mine are strong, something like Sam Shoemaker's near the end of his life: "I look back with many thanks.

It has been a great run. I wouldn't have missed it for anything." Ecclesiastes says it just right: "I have seen the business that God has given to the sons of men to be busy with. He has made everything beautiful in its time; also he has put eternity into man's mind" (3:10-11).

But let's not kid ourselves. We had better mix realisms with all that optimism. What are a few of them?

One. The church will rise again. She may be smaller, a purged, self-conscious minority taking her clues from Christ in self-giving, loving, and serving. Her temples will be less impressive and crucial, but her tasks more so. She will employ the interest and skills of youth (and the young in heart) to move mountains of prejudice, ignorance, and greed.

Two. We shall come to a lofty appraisal of our common humanity. There will be a lot of screeching and howling, but black power (and red, and tan, and yellow) will keep pushing us, saying, "Take me seriously." And rightly, too. We whites will be ashamed and penitent again and again because of our lateness and indifference.

Three. Peace will come, though ploddingly. Why? We are out of alternatives. Man will not be stupid or sinful enough to blow it totally. In peace, human rights, and a creditable church we shall have many new pioneers.

We live in an awesome and wonderful decade. Hopefully, we may have a new heaven and a new earth. Can we move into it with the faith of the promise of Patmos: "Behold, I make all things new" (Rev. 21:5)?

Three Bald Questions

MANY OF US are looking in new depth at our evangelistic witness and our method of inviting others to Christ. The concern is most healthy and most welcome.

I have in my hands three wallet-size booklets on personal evangelism. One is "Steps to Peace with God" (Billy Graham Association). Another is "Life Can Have Meaning" (Nazarene). The third is "Four Spiritual Laws" (Campus Crusade). It is easy to be critical of some of this material, but that is not a very helpful posture. Perhaps the biggest problem is to take the other person's words and technique and make them our own. I predict that we will move into this challenge, create or adapt material of our own, and enter upon a most rewarding time of witness and outreach.

Here is one man's approach. Frankly, he tries to let his invitation grow out of a relationship of authentic interest, warmth, and concern. He is not working a magical formula but facing a most serious encounter concerning destiny, engaging in honest dialogue and witnessing to his own commitment to Christ.

The atmosphere is one of mutual trust and seeking when the friend raises the three bald questions. First he asks, "Don't you realize God loves you and cares deeply about your life?" Second, "Aren't you tired of running from yourself and God?" Third, "Wouldn't this be a good time for us to pray together about your need?" Such wording may not be exactly yours, but it may be modified to give your sincere tone to it. Can you think of yourself asking these questions? Is it possible that more of our conversations of concern could turn a corner like this? Would we not usually receive affirmative answers to all three inquiries? Can we ask such honest questions without sounding pious and superior, mechanical and joyless, boorish and preacherish? If so, we are on our way to winning friends to Christ.

What text shall we use? There are many but two are most helpful: Revelation 3:20 and 1 John 1:9. Christ stands at the door of the heart and knocks. Will we hear his voice and open the door? If we confess our sins, God is faithful and will forgive our sins. The emphasis is clearly on man seeing his need and receiving new life in Christ.

The ideal, of course, is for the Christian witness to show concern beyond conversion. Can we see him on through the infilling of the Holy Spirit, baptism, and fellowship in the community of faith or will our casualness on follow-up make it an aborted mission?

The Man for Others

DIETRICH BONHOEFFER gives us a most helpful Holy Week lesson when he speaks of Christ as "the man existing for others, hence the crucified." Yes, if you are looking for the right peg on which to hang great meanings, think of our Lord as "The Man for Others."

We talk week after week to the young men and women in the Seminary about taking seriously the ministry of Jesus Christ. They say that Bonhoeffer's phrase has unusual appeal for them; it spells out their vocation. More specifically, they say that an authentic call to the Christian ministry involves an awareness of need, a conviction of capacity, and a willingness to serve. In so many ways they will "stand in the middle," the bridge over which God's forgiveness and peace may travel. They are given "the ministry of reconciliation" (2 Cor. 5:18). It is an awesome challenge to attempt to be the man for others.

It is small wonder that Dietrich Bonhoeffer has been an inspiration to our generation of young ministers. In 1931 he was a young student-pastor in Berlin. After Hitler's rise to power in 1933 and his vigorous persecution of the church, Bonhoeffer quietly founded a seminary in Finkenwalde. In 1937 Himmler ordered it closed. Bonhoeffer's friends urged him to leave the country until the war was over. He was tempted, came to New York for a few weeks in 1939. However, his conscience called him back, and he wrote on the eve of his departure: "I must live through this difficult period of our national history with the Christian people of Germany. I will have no right to participate in the reconstruction of Christian life in Germany after the war if I do not share the trials of this time with my people."

Bonhoeffer went back to Germany and engaged in an underground ministry until 1943. In April of that year he was arrested and imprisoned for two years. On April 9, 1945, by an order from Heinrich Himmler, the thirty-nine-year-old theologian was hanged outside Flossenburg prison. The words and deeds of the young German inspire us.

Think of Christ on Good Friday as "The Man for Others." As St. Paul says, "While we were yet sinners, Christ died for us" (Rom. 5:8). He "suffered for sins, the just for the unjust" (1 Pet. 3:18). Our Lord came to radically identify with the world of need, and to bear in his body its burden and suffering. This is the vicariousness to which we are called.

God's Guitars

WE HAD SOME toe-tapping music recently in Seminary. On two occasions, young guitarists, Gene Cotton and Mark Gough played and sang for us. I mused wonderingly that in the New Testament lists of the gifts of the Spirit (Rom. 12, 1 Cor. 12 and Eph. 4) music, much less guitar picking, is not listed. Sorry fellows!

A couple of years ago my daughters gave me a guitar for Christmas. I still can't play it. Small wonder that I marvel at the gift of the music instrumentalist. And there are many more gifts I marvel at. When I compare the first century list with ours of the twentieth, I rejoice at the range of God's anointing.

God's guitars get us going on one of the most timely and provocative doctrines in the Word of God. There is no question but that the Apostolic church was led and inspired by the gifted ones in the community of faith. Note 1 Corinthians 12:4-7. There were varieties of gifts. They were service gifts. They were for the common good. They were "for the equipment of the saints for the work of ministry" (Eph. 4:12). We have here the theological foundation of the *charisms* of the Spirit and the ministry of the whole people of God. This is what lay religion is all about.

One of the most teasing things about gifts is that they can be so diverse. At this point in my thinking I would be reluctant to put any limit on the human resources God can use to his glory. In fact, one's mind fairly does handsprings as it contemplates how the Holy Spirit may lay claim to man's talents and convert them into a style appropriate to the kingdom of God. This may be the most challenging and rewarding religious frontier ahead of us in the decade of the seventies. Surely eye has not seen and ear has not heard what God has prepared for those who love him, to pick up St. Paul's hope (1 Cor. 2:9). The challenge to all of us is to be alert and sensitive to what the Spirit is doing among Christians, and not to despise and condemn it.

Along with guitars, behold the way the barrier already is breached. To mention a few names is to be unfair to many other gifted ones, but the risk is worth it. I am impressed with Gene Sterner in proclamation, Mort Crim in communication, Frances Gardner Hunter in witness and writing, Bill Gaither in music composition. And that brings us full circle, back to guitars again. Let me as an old-timer make one soulful plea: Fellows, please turn down the tone my eardrums are bursting.

On Being "Both-and-ish"

WE HAVE A couple of options for reaction when we confront many of life's alternative positions. We may say that it is "either . . . or . . ." Also we may conclude that it is "both . . . and . . ." Do you have the same feeling I do that this latter option is one that has an increasing appeal? We are sometimes like the Kentucky evangelist who announced to his neighbor that the Lord was coming. The neighbor inquired, "When?" The preacher said, "It may be today and it may be tomorrow." The friend pleaded, "Don't tell my wife. She will want to go both days."

In the decade of the seventies we may yearn for the simple and the obvious, but not find them. The deeper meanings will come by keeping two truths in dynamic and creative tension, in learning a rhythm and alternation of our commitment. Believe it or not, there has been some recent slugging on the relative merits of personal conversion versus social action. My soul, when will we bury this battle? This one often points to the human gap between the fundamentalist and the liberal, or between the old and the young. It is in the solving of this conflict that I see how "both-and-ish" Jesus was. He kept both emphases. Read him carefully in John 3:15-18 and Luke 4:16-21. Why can't we weave the two thrusts—roots and fruits— into the gospel we preach?

Take other biblical examples. We may have a preference between faith and works. However, we are not given the authority to eliminate either (Jas. 2:14-18). Or look at Kingdom theology. As in no other doctrine, we must keep the seeming contradictions together. The kingdom of God inner *and* outer, *both* present *and* future, *both* personal *and* social, *both* silent *and* cataclysmic.

The doubleness of truth really comes home as we survey the two camps on churchly meanings: Is she fellowship or institution? We find our answer when we try to get along without either. She may be primarily fellowship, but, within history, she has always had form and structure. Yes, she is *both* commitment *and* committee, *both* mission *and* message, *both* action *and* agenda.

The young seminarian and minister asks, "Am I spokesman or servant, prophet or priest, thinker or technician?" The answer, loud and clear: "Both."

The many easy options have been too tempting. What a disservice to the Kingdom to think that we can choose between the altar and the arena, between worship and work, between the journey inward and the journey outward. The choice isn't that simple; it was not meant to be.

LET'S CELEBRATE

Soundings in Sentiment

Let's Celebrate

DO YOU HAVE the feeling, as I do, that we are not having enough fun in religion? Feasts and celebrations are a rarity in the realm of faith. There is considerable loss of zeal and enthusiasm. We still look for the fire, but we don't know where it is.

It was not always so. The Old Testament records great celebrations. Quick tabulations noted 112 references to trumpets blowing, 16 to cymbals, 26 to dancing. Here we have a mixture of instruments and actions utilized in praise of God. In our time they seem inappropriate.

Some ministers and churches, however, do some rather impressive celebrating. Every few weeks they have something to dedicate or commemorate. They will honor some person or some event with a memorial. They will dedicate a bus, a building, hymnals, new pews, a new billboard, and on and on. Frankly, I look upon this creativity as healthy for a congregation. If we are sensitive, we also can set up an Ebenezer or two saying, "Hitherto the Lord has helped us" (1 Sam. 7:12).

Is not corporate worship our best opportunity for celebration? This is where awareness of God's presence and blessings is keenest. The moods of tenderness, openness, and commitment are pervasive. Could we be more creative in employing all the senses in worship: sight, sound, smell, taste, and touch? They are God-given and could be used to open many more doors of meaning. The thought is staggering. We use *sound* mostly, and it is exploding with new tones of music. Praise of God will find many new avenues in the future.

Two facets of celebration interest us here. We might call them the first and second creation. First, note the wonderful world around us. (If it is spoiled, we did it.) Can we say Amen to the whole of God's creation? The joy of Sunday is to ratify the total range of God's gifts to us. It recapitulates the ancient Sabbath in celebrating God's mark of approval on the work he did for six days. Anything worth celebrating last week?

Next, the second creation. "If anyone is in Christ, he is a new creation" (2 Cor. 5:17). Here we celebrate the incarnation of God's Son and our new life in him. By redemption this second creation has rescued every thing from the bottomless abyss of sin. Our worship is joyous remembrance of our rescue. In our way we become redeeming, reconciling persons, men and women for others. When I think of it, my heart leaps for joy; should other parts of my anatomy follow? One, two, let's celebrate!

Dad—Gone Home

OUR DAD DIED today—November 2. He had critical heart damage ten days ago. When Chuck and I visited him in the hospital, he said he wanted to go home. We were not quite sure if he meant the place on Harrisonville Avenue or the Father's house. In either case he couldn't lose. He had been inspired by many readings of John 14:2: "In my Father's house are many rooms; . . . I go to prepare a place for you."

When the 2:30 A.M. telephone call told of dad's passing, there were the first shock and tears. But not for long. Many fine memories, scriptures, and even a poem flooded in. I thought of Vachel Lindsay's "General William Booth Enters into Heaven." The trumpets blow and the flags wave at the home-going of the saints. The days following dad's home-going, including Pastor Dale Lehman's memorial service in the church, were a celebration of dad's victory.

Dad, and his family, owe a lot to the church. He was converted forty years ago under Raymond Black's ministry. He served as teacher, trustee, treasurer, visitor. His retirement years brought him to a ministry of calling on the ill and shut-in. His prayer for healing was welcomed by all. So, like many laymen in the church, dad found joyous witness and fulfillment.

His immediate family, thirty-two in number, met for a private memorial service before going to the church. Our prayer was one of thanksgiving for a rich heritage and tradition. We read with Isaiah: "Look to the rock from which you were hewn, and to the quarry from which you were digged. Look to Abraham your father" (51:1-2a). Wife, children, and grandchildren worshiped and covenanted together to continue the household of faith.

At death, we need only one chapter really: First Corinthians 15. It helps us affirm the great doctrine of the Christian hope. Christ's resurrection has become the "first fruits" (v. 20) of those who sleep. He is our example, our guarantee. Death is brutally real and final: it is the "last enemy" (v. 26). But beyond it is the miracle of the resurrection. We are given a body fit for the new world of the spirit (v. 44). We are ushered into a larger, brighter room; the drama continues on a cosmic stage. The God relationship continues. All limiting factors (damaged heart) are removed. "Death is swallowed up in victory" (v. 54). God gives it "through . . . Jesus Christ" (v. 57). He shall reign (v. 25), giving heaven its distinction and its joy.

Welcome, Angela!

WILL YOU PLEASE indulge Agnes and me the privilege of this public celebration of our first grandchild? We do it in the name of all grandparents. Please forgive our condescension to all those who have not reached this lofty station. It takes patience and waiting.

Kay and David's daughter, Angela Christine, was born on Sunday, and that's a good omen. Remember the couplet: "And a child that is born on the Lord's day, is fair and wise and good and gay." But, born on any day, we would wish that for the cuddly infant in any home.

Let me tell you, grandparents are nuttier than anybody. They are hit by emotions they had almost forgotten. They say foolish things, make rash promises, brag like captains. They know that Proverbs is right: "Grandchildren are the crown of old age, and sons are proud of their fathers" (17:6, NEB).

Add to that a most sobering verse from Deuteronomy: "I punish the children for the sins of the fathers to the third and fourth generations of those who hate me. But I keep faith with thousands, with those who love me and keep my commandments" (5:9-10, NEB). Yes, grandfathers are being weighed in the balances of God. The continuity of life in families is both God's gift and God's lesson.

Now, may I talk to Angela a moment? My dear, let me applaud your parents. They wanted you and planned for you. Please forgive their nervousness and ineptness these first few days. Parents learn fast. You would be flattered and laugh if you could hear a recording some day of all their nursery talk. The worst they call you is "a little tax deduction," the best is heavenly.

Next, let me applaud the doctors and nurses. They work with such wisdom, efficiency, and tenderness. In your nursery were some "preemies" who were getting the same

T.L.C. you were. The hospital staff works so feelingly with God's strategy to give and prolong life. You may find yourself someday in a vocation like theirs.

Angela, I wish we might applaud appropriately the religious experience we have had in all this. I am talking about faith and gratitude. It will take a poet and musician to do them justice. It seems that when a meal needs cooking, a dress needs sewing, a house needs building, an atmosphere needs purifying, a truth needs telling, a wrong needs righting, God sends a baby into the world. Welcome! Remember, grandpa gets to buy the first ice-cream cone.

Dear Beth

WE KICKED you out of the nest this past September and sent you off to college. You are the third, and last, to go. So we celebrated!

How did we feel about it? You were a little scared, but excited. Mother and I were a little sad, but glad. We owed it to ourselves to let you go, for this is the goal toward which we have striven. Though you have been with us, you do not belong to us.

Yes, we celebrated this September. However, the experience was a teasing one. Let me speak for the dads who were full of sentiment "up to here" as daughters drove off to college. We touched hands and cheek as you left. The first time we did that, you were only hours old. You do not remember, but I do. I see you as a three-year-old with a cuddly kitten in your arms; as a six-year-old learning to ride your bike; as a nine-year-old tooting a flute-o-phone; as a twelve-year-old going to youth camp. Then came the junior high wonder years of buzz saw energy. But, if anything, the pace quickened after fifteen. There were dental braces and contact lenses, new books

64

and magazines by the ton, drama and music at church and school, the new guitar, first dates, camps, conventions, parties, trips, jobs, sewing, baking, gabbing, and finally, whirlwind senior activities. Beth, we wouldn't have missed it for anything. Please forgive us for being a bit sentimental.

Beth, believe it or not, the best is yet to be. You are an adult now. Your mental powers are as great as they will ever be. You are capable of great sensitivity, great courage, great commitment. The new ingredient is that you are no longer an echo, but your own voice. You have grown into your own individuality. These are now *your* insights, *your* decisions, *your* pressures, *your* world. Welcome to the club!

What can the college freshman reasonably expect of herself? (Here's dad still giving advice.) Apparently, the freedom to enter the doors of wisdom, beauty, joy, and service which are flung open. Apparently, the determination to live with oneself, to take the consequences of one's acts, to combine responsibility with freedom. Apparently, the dedication to carve out a vocation that will be both honoring to God and fulfilling to man. You will do these, and your example and encouragement will help dad and mother do them better.

Beth, we take your desire to leave the nest and be independent as a compliment to us. Fly, dear one, fly!

Jerusalem, My Home

THE HOLY LAND is really quite unholy now, but Jerusalem, the capital, is still the Golden City. Six of us were there recently. The sights, sounds, and smells are now quite familiar. There was not a futurist or literalist among us—that is, in terms of the enthronement of a new David in a spiritual kingdom, or a final clash of men and arms in the plains around Megiddo. And the fashioning of holy places around celebrated sites made us a bit sick. (We would like to tear down a few cathedrals.) However, all of us fell in love with Jerusalem.

One can make music about her, as did the psalmist: "His holy mountain, beautiful in elevation, is the joy of all the earth, Mount Zion . . . the city of the great King. Walk about Zion, go round about her . . . Consider well" her walls and buildings (Ps. 48:2, 12-13). Or one can weep over her, as Jesus did (Luke 19:41).

A Jordanian restaurant operator, driven out by the war said, "She's the greatest; I must return." A Jewish physician told me, "I would live nowhere else." That's what the Moslem and Jew said. What does the Christian say, not forgetting that the city is sacred to all?

Why is Jerusalem my home? The Christian reacts more theologically and historically. First, he develops a doctrine of continuity. In a small compass of land the drama of the Old and New Testaments was acted out. It is at once the home of David, of Solomon, of Jesus, of Paul. The magnificent Dome of the Rock which today dominates the temple area is the Mount Moriah where Abraham was ready to sacrifice Isaac. This is the location of Solomon's temple and later, Herod's, where Jesus drove out the money changers. The old and the new overlay each other.

Second, we have a wonderful historical tapestry of place and people. God chose a race for covenant with himself, and then one from among them to represent him totally. This is where it happened; this is where Jesus became one of us. One stands beside Jacob's well where our Lord met the woman of Samaria. One stands in the pool of Siloam where Jesus sent the blind man to wash the clay from his eyes. Yes, literally one walks where Jesus walked. Christianity is not fiction but glorious history.

One weeps again for the city as did the daughters of Jerusalem on Jesus' fateful day (Luke 23:28). Arab and Jew are political rivals, and Jerusalem is again the victim. Pray with me for the Golden City, our spiritual home.

"An Eagle Remembered"

I WAS IN THE SIXTH grade when hero worship came home to me in the person of Charles A. Lindbergh. Forty years ago this May, the Lone Eagle crossed the Atlantic in a single-engine plane. From that time, many boys like myself read, talked, and sang about Lindbergh. We, no doubt, had heroes and heroines in history and fiction, but here was one in flesh and blood.

On May 21, 1927 Lindbergh took off from New York and, after 33 hours alone in the cockpit of his plane, the *Spirit of St. Louis,* hurtling through canyons of clouds and storm, over 3,600 miles of ocean, landed at Le Bourget Field, Paris. This was the first nonstop flight between the continents of America and Europe. The flight was an engineering and navigational feat; it was also an emotional and spiritual victory. Lindbergh said in his autobiography, "It's hard to be an agnostic up here in the *Spirit of St. Louis,* aware of the frailty of man's devices, a part of the universe between its earth and stars." Lindbergh (now in his sixties and living in Darien, Conn.) became a legend in his lifetime.

Of what stuff are heroes made? Note with me a few ingredients. First, they call on deep inner resources of courage and creativity. Second, they are indifferent to credit and praise. Third, they take their place as dedicated citizens, contributing largely to the common good. Note, typically, that Lindbergh refused to have any part in ceremonies celebrating the 40th anniversary of his flight.

67

Will you pick a few heroes and heroines with me? I would take Moses and Esther in the Old Testament, Barnabas and Lydia in the New. How do you like John Glenn and Gus Grissom among the astronauts? Billy Graham and Catherine Marshall in religion? Dwight Eisenhower and Eleanor Roosevelt in public life? Carl Erskine and Althea Gibson in sports? Charles Schulz and Marian Anderson in the arts? Let the list continue: Helen Keller, Jane Addams, John Kennedy, Dag Hammarskjold, Kagawa, Schweitzer, Tom Dooley, Pearl Buck, Dale Evans.

I can read Hebrews 11 and 12 and get pretty sentimental about the great biblical heroes. Yes, we are surrounded "by a great cloud of witnesses." The lesson for the moment is an affirmation that pioneering and serving are not in the past. We shall continue to praise and copy the authentic hero. Lives of great men all remind us. If we need a text, I would point to Luke 12:48: "To whom much is given, of him will much be required; and of him to whom men commit much, they will demand the more."

Forgetting

FOR THE SAKE of their spiritual health, Christians ought to be good forgetters. Let the new year be mainly a time of looking ahead. Why can't we drop things in the sea of forgetfulness, as God does?

The Lord said to Moses, ". . . Tell the people of Israel to go forward" (Exod. 14:15, RSV). Maybe the musical theme from the drama *Exodus* would inspire us, as it does our youth, if we played it this new year. Forgetting the losses and oppressions of Egypt, respond to the call of Canaan.

This turning around and changing direction is the biblical doctrine of repentance. We Christians know that God helps us do this as a master decision at the beginning of our walk with him. In all humility, we also know that there should be some annual repeating of it. Let the family turn away from the hurts, the neighborhood from the scars, the church from the disappointments. We do this, not by massive animal force, but by letting all these be covered by divine and human forgiveness. This is the spiritual chemistry of forgetting.

Abraham Maslow points to our problem at the new year this way, "We cling to safety and defensiveness out of fear, tending to regress backward, hanging on to the past, afraid to grow. . . ." We can understand and accept children and fear-ridden pagans who hang on to the past, but it is not healthy for adult, emancipated Christians to do so.

Christians have so much to go forward to. Think with me of three. We are called ahead to peace, to unity, to service. There are many more, but these are so substantial and so worthy. Can we get a running start on them this month? Think of our promises, our riches as Christians as this year of our Lord is ushered in! Join with me in singing lustily the theme from *Exodus*. Like Paul, let us pledge: "Forgetting what lies behind, we press on."

Maslow is right: Too often we are "afraid to grow." He says we are committed to the safety factor rather than the growth factor. In the choice between giving up safety or giving up growth, safety usually wins out. Of all persons Christians ought to be most free to grow. As the poet enjoins, "Leave thy low vaulted past, ... till thou art free"—free to grow.

CRUCIFIED BY STUPIDITY
Soundings in the Christian Year

Crucified by Stupidity

WHILE WE are still in the mood of Easter and the resurrection, let us say a good word for rational Christianity. One writer has said that Jesus was crucified by stupidity. He bases this on that word from the cross: "Father, forgive them; for they know not what they do" (Luke 23:34).

We have the stupidity of the closed mind (Pilate); the false choice ("release Barabbas"); the short look (the whole city of Jerusalem that week). Isn't it amazing that the city and her leaders could have gone that mad in so short a time? But before we become too judgmental let us remind ourselves how easy it is for us to lose perspective, engage in foggy dialogue, and be guilty of thickheadedness. Is it fair to say that we too crucify our Lord by our stupidity? When we sing "Were you there . . . ?" we know we must say yes.

The emotions and the intellect are both involved in Christian experience. The first is more simple and automatic, the second is more difficult. To love God "with all your mind" (Mark 12:30) is a most commanding challenge. To read some of the literature of our time or to listen to some of the cults and independents is to have one's intelligence insulted. There is fantastic obscurantism regarding the signs of the times, the role of the Jews, or prophecy concerning the Middle East, to name a few. Is it too much to expect that our biblical interpretation, program, and strategies should make good sense? Why should the sons of this world be wiser in their own generation than the sons of light? (Luke 16:8). The unbeliever has no monopoly on intelligence. Anti-intellectualism is not one of the gifts of the Spirit, but knowledge and wisdom are (1 Cor. 12:8). In these challenging times I would plead for an obstinate rationality and toughmindedness.

This appeal is not to glamorize the schoolman or celebrity intellectual. Rather it is to argue for insight, discernment, sensitivity, diplomacy, and communication. We cannot panic mentally and spiritually in the face of all new assaults on the faith. Let's hold steady. In the counsel of many there is wisdom.

People were asking in ancient Jerusalem and they are asking today, "Is Jesus Christ trustworthy?" We would be scandalized if we thought we were crucifying him by our stupidity. Now is just the right time to give an answer and a reason for our faith (1 Pet. 3:15).

Easter: Magnificent Simplicity

EASTER, that is, the Christian celebration of the cross and the empty tomb, is not all that difficult. The eyes of trust see great meaning and hope in them. They may not bend to logic, but they do to faith.

What is the simple lesson? It tells us of God, the initiator. It says that man no longer has to search for God; God has searched for man, and found him. This is the point where we link Easter with Christmas, the cross with the crib, atonement with incarnation. At the cross we see the purpose of God entering history as Mary's baby boy.

We have a word which conveys the simple message of Easter. It is *reconciliation.* It is the bringing together of God and man in a union of peace. Look at the problem again. Man knows himself to be in a state of prideful rebellion against his Creator, the lover of his soul. The relationship is fractured. Man is the loner, the loser, the leaver of God. God will not settle for this and moves toward us in love. As Paul puts it, "God was in Christ reconciling."

If sin is the refusal of God's love, then the cross illustrates the extent to which God will go, in suffering love, to bridge our refusal. As *Good News for Modern Man* puts it, "All this is done by God, who through Christ changed us from enemies into his friends, and gave us the task of making others his friends also" (2 Cor. 5:18). Christ's enemies, religious and political, did their worst to him. They murdered him shamefully. He uttered not a "mumblin' word." Now, no person can treat this deed casually. Behold Calvary! The stony places of our heart are broken up as we behold the selfless act.

Yes, God did act. The enormity of human sin required it. Our rebellion was a scandal to God's holiness. We are not talking so much about a price paid as a process followed. God had to settle the issue of man's alienation. He was requiring much, but also giving much. What his nature demanded, his love provided, namely, the sacrifice of his son. This is the pattern by which God and man can once again become "at-one"—reconciled. Paul put it, "For if while we were enemies we were reconciled to God by the death of his Son, much more, now that we are reconciled, shall we be saved by his life" (Rom. 5:10).

How does Christ become effective for me? By faith, I dip into the great reservoir of forgiveness established by his cross. It is that simple.

Pentecost: Making Christ Current

JESUS IS NOT walking on earth now, but somehow his work goes forward; somehow his Spirit marches on. That's it! After Christ, came the great and abiding activity of the

Holy Spirit. Get the picture? Just hours after Christ had ascended to the Father, his followers were meeting in homes, recalling his words, singing his praises, planning his work. Though he was physically absent, he was feelingly, really present in the Spirit. Had he not said, "Lo, I am with you always" (Matt. 28:20)?

The infant church made the transition from the physical to the spiritual Presence beautifully. If anything, they were more sensitive and disciplined, for now they communed with Christ at the deepest and realest level, namely the spiritual. Best of all, he could be in all hearts and homes at once. This is the lesson we will address ourselves to this Pentecost. May it happen again!

The truth we are talking about is the *paraclete* or "comforter" doctrine given us in John, chapters 14 to 16. I remember personally how this great lesson came to me some years ago through the instruction of Dr. Paul S. Rees. I shall be eternally thankful, for I take it to be close to the heart of the gospel, surely of Pentecost.

Drink deeply of this truth with me: The Spirit is the reminder, the continuer of the finished work of Christ. Our Lord promised that "when the Comforter is come . . . even the Spirit of truth . . . he shall testify of me" (John 15:26). Moreover, "He will declare to you the things that are to come. He will glorify me, for he will take what is mine and declare it to you" (John 16:13-14).

Line on line the promises come, and they put iron in our blood for today's battles. "These things I have spoken to you, while I am still with you. But the Counselor, the Holy Spirit, whom the Father will send in my name, he will teach you all things, and bring to your remembrance all that I have said to you" (John 14:25-26). There we have it. If Christ is to be our contemporary, the Holy Spirit will make him so.

O Beautiful for Patriot Dream

I SAW IT again today, that placard on an automobile which read, "America, Love It or Leave It." I felt the same emotion again, as always: distress, bordering upon anger. Why? Because I refuse to accept those as the only two alternatives. I am not about to leave America. On the other hand, there are some things my nation is doing right now that I dislike intensely. So I reserve the right to criticize.

Patriotism has become a "No, no" for many youth and some adults. It seems to me the time has come to make it noble and meaningful again. Surely there are worthy and unworthy patriotisms. They vary from sensitive devotion to emotional lunacy. Our flag is a provocative symbol, though it is rather incidental to patriotism. I will not worship it, though I surely respect it. One has to see it waving over the American Embassy in Moscow to have that ultimate kind of feeling of commitment.

To me patriotism means that I love my country's good, I wish her well, and I will do my part to make her noble. It is not a short and frenzied outburst of emotion, for or against. Rather it has the steady dedication of a lifetime. There is great profundity in Jesus' statement in Mark 12:17: "Render unto Caesar the things that are Caesar's, and to God the things that are God's."

Where shall we challenge "Caesar"? At two points right now. We made a monumental goof in getting involved in a civil war in the far East and supporting a corrupt government of one of the participants. And, second, we are moving so belatedly and slowly in achieving human rights for all our citizens, particularly minorities. Our patriotic duty is to stay with the ship and be responsible Christians until these wrongs are righted. Indeed, like Jefferson, we may feel, "I tremble for my country when I reflect that God is just."

Remember the text. We surely will not allow Caesar to seize the things which are God's. The patriot's dream is that devotion to God and country will continue as our birthright and sacred trust.

Let Us Break Bread Together

DO WE NEED to be reminded that World Communion Sunday comes each October? With the exception of the Quakers, most denominations will celebrate. It is one ceremony which brings us in Christendom close to each other and to Christ. That makes it worth all the attention we give.

Let us state the case. The Lord's Supper is the memorial meal established by Christ (Matt. 26:26-29), and practiced by the early church (1 Cor. 11:24-26) the first day of the week (Acts 20:7). It is also called "Communion" (1 Cor. 10:16) and the "Lord's Table." It commemorates Christ's death for sin, celebrates communion and fellowship with the living Lord, and proclaims his Second Coming (1 Cor. 11:26). All Christians should partake of this feast regularly (Acts 20:7) and reverently (1 Cor. 11:27-29). Such a biblical base is more than enough to move us toward a rather profound theology for our breaking of bread.

I like to think of the communion meditation as a "Table Talk." In my life I have heard some inspiring ones. For example, there is the "Come and dine" emphasis. We are served "refreshments." We are nourished in body, mind, and spirit at the table. Bread, the commonest commodity, speaks of our being strengthened by the living Christ. The Allied armies during World War II gathered up hungry, homeless children. That night they were restless and afraid. Finally a psychologist put a piece of bread in their hand at bedtime—not to eat, but to hold. They knew they had something to eat tomorrow. Think of the deep, deep level at which we celebrate Jesus as the Bread of Life for all our tomorrows.

Think of the table talks on celebration. There are all kinds. Perhaps we celebrate best with the very literal symbols of the bread and the cup. They convey a memorial of meanings, a covenant of companionship, a continuity of grace, a pledge of love. Let World Communion rekindle the flame of our commitment. It can be the bread of thanksgiving and the cup of joy.

I like those talks on confidence and hope, "until he comes." That phrase in 1 Corinthians 11:26 is one of the most weighty and suggestive in Scripture. It announces our posture, our program, our Christian life-style. With the bread and with the cup, we proclaim the Lord's death until he comes. We sing and serve, preach and pray, worship and work, hope and heal, until he comes.

God Is for Us—Be Thankful

A FAMILY I know has the custom of beginning long out of town and vacation trips by stopping the car at the city limits and offering a prayer to God. They conclude the trip the same way. This family exercise is as good an example as I know of the doctrine of grace. It acknowledges that God is with us and God is for us. In the setting of the automobile and travel it might be called prevenient or "preventing" grace. It says that God's power is present to sharpen, to quicken, to assist our driving, our reflexes, our journey as a whole. It is putting the emphasis in the right place, for when we travel we should go with God.

That modest word "grace" is perhaps the most crucial concept in Christian theology because it refers to the free and unmerited act through which God restores his estranged creatures to himself. In the Old Testament the word means literally "favor." In the New Testament grace refers to the freely given redeeming action of God through Christ.

St. Paul wrestled with this meaning and gave his classic statement: "For by grace you have been saved through faith; and this is not your own doing, it is the gift of God —not because of works, lest any man should boast" (Eph. 2:8-9). Salvation is not wages and is not for sale; it is God's gift. Can you think of any greater cause for thanksgiving this November?

Earlier Paul says, "He destined us in love to be his sons through Jesus Christ" (Eph. 1:5). It is God himself, not an impersonal thing or proposition, in his goodwill toward men. It is God resolving to be for man, to be present to him despite his rebelliousness.

A recent book title tries to shock us into paying appropriate attention to grace. It is R. Lofton Hudson's *Grace Is Not a Blue-Eyed Blond*. He says, "God is like the sea, ebbing and flowing into each of us according to our needs and accessibility." That is grace. Paul Tournier speaks of it as the "all-inclusive and unconditional love." It is God, whose capacity for giving is inexhaustible, acting out of his deepest being. So, this November, we have little excuse for boasting. Believing in the Creator and Father of us all, we can only give glory and thanks to God.

We have God's supporting and strengthening activity; be thankful. We have God's saving and protecting activity; be thankful. God is for us; be thankful.

Advent: God in Civilian Clothes

OUR MADISON County Sheriff, John Gunter, is a Christian layman. Recently he had to deliver some convicted youths to Plainfield Boy's School. He invited parents and friends to visit them the day before they left. At the end of the day he walked down the cellblock and one of the boys said, "Sheriff, no one visited me." John said, "I will." He went home, changed to civilian clothes, and came back with his guitar. He unlocked the door and took the youth to the basement of the jail where they talked and sang and ate popcorn.

This exciting little incident hit me like lightning. I have never heard a better analogy of incarnation. At Bethlehem God became a visitor to our planet; he put on civilian clothes and joined us. Through the Holy Spirit we can talk and sing and eat together. As the Fourth Gospel puts it, "The Word became flesh and dwelt among us" (1:14).

The incarnation is the sublime mystery of our faith. We can only experience it, not explain it. Yet it is a well-rounded story. God got himself, not only embodied, but also expressed—expressed in the wonderful life and character of our Lord. Advent is the time of the year to contemplate deeply and feelingly on the God who put on civilian clothes.

Let our meditating on this truth give us hope. Just as the "Word made flesh" came into that fractured and ugly world of the first century, he comes into ours. The incarnation says that the glory of God can be revealed in the little place and the everyday event. In common times and in crisis times, he comes.

Here is his word on it: "I have come that they may have life, and have it abundantly" (John 10:10). He came to dwell among us, and in us. Our very bodies become his temples. The challenge of Advent is to affirm life, to say yes to life. St. Irenaeus (second century) wrote inspiringly of the God in civilian clothes: "The Word of God, Jesus Christ, on account of his great love for mankind, became what we are in order to make us what he is himself."

Christmas: Rachel Weeps for Her Children

IS IT APPROPRIATE this Christmas to look at the furious rage of Herod as he killed all the male children in order to get rid of competing kings? This was the insane part of the Bethlehem event. Matthew 2:18 quotes Jeremiah: "A voice was heard in Ramah, wailing and loud lamentation, Rachel weeping for her children; she refused to be consoled, because they were no more."

Christmas each year will be hard on Christians. Why? It will be difficult to cut through all the trappings to the authentic light, joy, and peace. We are as inhospitable as the innkeeper to the babe of Bethlehem. We are insensitive to the meaning of God's mighty act.

However, I for one will not give up. Will you confess with me Christ's glorious incarnation? Will you walk with me toward the light as did the shepherds of Bethlehem? Will you sing the *Gloria in Excelsis,* as the angels did?

Let us look at the heart of the matter again. Christmas and the incarnation say that God is now a part of the world in which we live. Man no longer has to search for God; God has searched for man, and found him. The world is the stage and Christ took the role of a servant on it. He shares our problems and concern; he knows our pain. He became the involved God and invites us to involvement. So the kingdom of God has come among us.

St. Paul put it so well: "When the fullness of the time was come, God sent forth his Son . . . to redeem them" (Gal. 4:4-5). Is it possible that our weeping and yearning are for a new fullness of time? A time when we may again receive light, joy, and peace?

Receive light. At our Lord's birth the night was filled with heavenly radiance. He still lightens the thick darkness of the world and the gloom of our miseries and fears. May he rekindle our hearts anew. *Receive light.*

Receive joy. The angel said, "Be not afraid; . . . I bring you good news of a great joy" (Luke 2:10). Let us ask if our Christmas really could be merry and touched with joy divine. Since Christ came not to condemn but to redeem, it really could. *Receive joy.*

Receive peace. The song again: "Glory to God in the highest, and on earth peace" (Luke 2:14). It is still our dream that persons and nations in sorrow and desolation may find peace in Christ's presence and comfort in his love. *Receive peace.*

Christmas: Try Giving Yourself Away

AT CHRISTMAS TIME Ralph Waldo Emerson throws a wonderful caution at us: "Rings and jewels are not gifts, but apologies for gifts. The only gift is a portion of thyself." How about that?

Some religious groups are very critical about the celebrating we do at Christmas because some of it has pagan origins. Well, most of us are unhappy about the intruding paganisms, old and new. The giving and receiving of gifts is a good place to start redeeming them, especially as we learn that it is when we give of ourself that we truly give.

Actually, giving is quite appropriate as we recall the incarnation. "God so loved the world that he gave" (John 3:16). The wise men brought those memorable gifts of gold, frankincense, and myrrh to the Christ child (Matt. 2:11).

Look how symbolic those ancient gifts were. Gold refers to the substantial and priceless sharing of energy, time and talents. Frankincense is the perfume and sweetness of enthusiasm and concern. Myrrh was the pungent gum used in burial ceremonies and recalls deep commitment and sacrifice. Thus the tangible gifts may convey deep lessons and meanings.

But let's move to the intangible gifts and experience the more ultimate truth that the gift without the giver is bare. Think of imparting the treasures of charitableness and gratitude, courage and concern, thoughtfulness and responsibility, courtesy and enthusiasm, kindness and sympathy, joy and hope. These truly are priceless.

One Christmas our daughter Jill had less than enough money for the presents she wanted to give the family. We received neatly wrapped and ribboned messages such as these: *Good for two car washes. Good for two floor scrubbings.* Talk about a sentimental time and a precious memory!

If we put our minds to it, we could think of our own list of unbuyable gifts. As we share them, we would come into Christian adventure and Yuletide gaiety never experienced before. It would be worthy of the memory of the total self-giving of our Lord.

A DIRTY LITTLE RIVER TOWN
Soundings in the Now

A Dirty Little River Town

I WAS INTRODUCED once as being a resident of a "dirty little river town" (New Boston, Ohio), and I resented it. Within the last month I flew over the town and also approached it from the east in a car—and you know what? It *is* a dirty little river town! A division of Detroit Steel is located there, and a pall of brown smoke hangs over the river valley. And, like the other towns up and down the river, the refuse from the disposal plants flows into the Ohio River.

Recall that inspiring sentence in Genesis 1 after the word of creation was spoken: "And God saw that it was good" (vv. 12, 18, 22). Yes, it was good, and man has been the spoiler. Pollution has sneaked up on us. The ravaging of the earth has been going on for scores of years, but only in recent months have we been awakened to its consequences. Life on this planet literally is in jeopardy. It took "Earth Day" (April 22) to awaken all of us to the seriousness of the problem. Many of us still don't believe it, and still are spoilers.

And, there still are jokes. Mayor Lindsay of New York said he refused to breathe anything he couldn't see. The man from South Charleston, visiting in the country, said he wanted to get back to the Kanawha Valley "where the air had body to it." But we are kidding on facts and it is sick humor.

Why should we raise the question of pollution and does the church have a word to say on it? These are the questions. Many will find it new and difficult to think of the gospel as encompassing them. Others, including the writer, will agree with William Temple that "God is concerned about many things, in addition to religion."

Pollution is pretty rangy, isn't it? It occurs in the mind, the body, the community, as well as the environment. Touching the latter, we have the psalmist's word on it: "The earth is the Lord's and the fulness thereof, the world and those who dwell therein" (24:1). We, our children and our brethren, are "those who dwell therein." That's us he's talking about, and we are precious in his sight. The whole man is under the divine concern, and what he breaths, drinks, and eats. It must not be poison.

Shall the minister and the church invest their word, their influence and power, in the pollution problem? They are considerable and they would be heard. They could make the universe sacramental again. "This is my Father's world!"

The Shape of Adam's Rib

"WAS ST. PAUL married?" asked the professor. "I think so," said the student, "because he tells us about his thorn in the flesh."

Such a joke never was very good humor, but especially now when women's liberation is being debated. Can we approach the problem from the viewpoint of both good sense and good religion and leave jokes and prejudice behind us? Most all men have this prejudice, and, believe it or not, many women do. Many women would vote negative if the pulpit committee presented a female.

Our church has a striking early record on the leadership of women. Of the persons listed in the book, *Familiar Names and Faces* (1902), one-third were women. All of us can bring names of ordained women preachers who had led and inspired us. But the list now is the smallest it has ever been.

St. Paul states a clear and elevated rank for women in the church: "There is neither Jew nor Greek, there is neither slave nor free, their is neither male nor female; for you are all one in Christ Jesus" (Gal. 3:28). One can state the case for the liberation for the whole of mankind (?) from that text.

The two juicy texts for the suppression of women are also from Paul. "They are not permitted to speak, but should be subordinate" (1 Cor. 14:34). "I permit no woman to teach or to have authority over men; she is to keep silent" (1 Tim. 2:12). Thus the oft-quoted base for the silent, subordinate role.

But that interpretation will not wash. Paul is not stating for us a natural or divine law, but rather a Jewish cultic and synagogue law. It grows out of cultural and social meanings rather than spiritual and human. It needs to be updated and made applicable to the twentieth century. The low position of women (as in Hebrew society) may be made high and noble. But all of us will have to work at it. How about starting a grand strategy for it now?

I like Charles Wesley's stanzas:

> *Not from his head was woman took,*
> *As made her husband to o'erlook.*
> *Not from his feet, as one designed*
> *The footstool of the stronger kind,*
> *But fashioned for himself a bride;*
> *An equal, taken from his side.*

It is time to get over the hangup of women doing most of the work of the church, while men exercise most of the authority.

On Being Tuned In

CAN FINITE man be tuned to the Infinite? is a question old and young are asking with deep earnestness. The Christian faith answers in the affirmative. We profess that God is always touching us by claim and promise.

"Tuning in" is not a bad way to put it. God gives the signal. He calls; man replies. God initiates; man responds. God acts; man reacts. This is the heartening doctrine of grace. A statement of it is Psalm 56:9c: "God is for me."

We have to be brutal here about the radical distinctives of God. There is nothing of creatureliness in him. The being of God and the being of creatures is totally different. It probably is not possible to elevate his sovereignty too high. We stand in awe, and bow in reverence before him. Young Isaiah "saw the Lord sitting upon a throne, high and lifted up" (6:1). His response was the only appropriate one: "Holy, holy, holy is the Lord of hosts; the whole earth is full of his glory" (v. 3). "Woe is me! For I am lost" (v. 5). Here, in the context of worship, is the account of God's otherness, his transcendence.

How, pray tell, with such an exalted doctrine of God, can we speak of being tuned in? There is only one hope, one window, one link. It is the doctrine of the image of God in man. It says that, though God is totally unlike us, he has invested a contact point in man with which he can communicate. Genesis 1 tells the remarkable story: "Let us make man in our image, after our likeness" (v. 26).

What does it mean? We may not be intelligent enough to know really, but our faith and spiritual instincts give some reassurance. They say that basically man is non-physical, more akin to mind than matter. The image of God tells us, with Augustine, that we are made *for* God and are restless until we rest in him. And it says that we are invested with a joyous (and frightening) freedom. It is our most heavenly credential.

Tuning in does not require the hokeyness of drugs, strobe lights, and psychedelic chambers, fortunately. They are much too selective. And that's trying too hard.

Tuning in means *celebrating in, by, with,* and *through* God. By repentance and faith we are putting our whole existence under his authority. We are open to God and to each other, delighted in elemental simplicities, and surprised by joy.

On Being Turned On

I HEAR many say they have a sense of life being unlived and unfulfilled. Yet they still hold to the promise of God in creation "Be fruitful and multiply, and fill the earth and subdue it; and have dominion—" (Gen. 1:28). We continue to ask seriously, What is it that opens us up and turns us on?

One wonders if our Lord asked a similar question as he presented himself by the Jordan, at the age of thirty, for John's baptism. There followed the terrifying temptations in the real world. Soon after he returned to his hometown to go to work. He addressed family and community in the synagogue: "The Spirit of the Lord is upon me, . . . to preach good news . . . to proclaim release . . . recovering of sight . . . to set at liberty . . . to proclaim the acceptable year of the Lord" (Luke 4:18). What an announcement; what a platform! Jesus moved into the world, which God has not forsaken, to be God's man and God's servant.

What turned Jesus on? He undoubtedly had a supreme God-consciousness which prompted total obedience. He was sensitive to the needs of people and he cared (he cried over Jerusalem). He responded to the servant vocation and lived it out, Kingdom style. The question we shall continue to ask is whether such qualities and credentials will turn us on.

Sincere Christians strive for an integrity and an authenticity. Somehow they would like not only to bring a truth, but *be* a truth; not only to bring good news but to *be* good news. Here is a transparent witness, the very incarnation of love and service.

Are we correct that laymen are looking for relevance and involvement? Are they asking for a definition of their ministry? Are they inquiring what will tune them in and turn them on? Apparently they are. This appraisal of the whole church ministering to the whole world is one of the most heartening developments in our time. It points us toward renewal. It emphasizes the utilization of gifts by all God's children as Paul does in First Corinthians 12. This is the word and the truth through which they are sanctified (John 17:17).

Our good fortune is that we serve a calling-sending God. He invites us to a rhythm of challenge and response, of meditation and service, of gathering and scattering. He does not coerce, but he surely tempts and teases to emancipation and aliveness.

Stop the World!

BROADWAY HAD an interesting play title: Stop the *World, I Want to Get Off!* Who hasn't felt like saying that occasionally? Events are moving too fast. Experiences are too different. Happenings are too frightening. The ultimate of disenchantment with the world would be to go the route of suicide.

A touching example of cultural world-stopping came to our state this month as several Amish families in northern Indiana packed up and moved to Missouri. The hauling was done by others, for the Amish will not use modern equipment and utilities. Their children are not permitted to attend public schools. Can we say, charitably, that they appear to want to stop the clock in the mid-nineteenth century? They prefer the social, scientific, and cultural world decades ago in rural America.

Billy Graham and Ralph Sockman debated the "old-time religion" on the radio. Many guessed that it would be a slugfest between a conservative and a liberal. They were surprised at the unusual agreement between the two: They like the old-time religion only if it is "old enough," that is, first century, Christly, and apostolic. They refused to stop and freeze the religious world in the nineteenth century or the sixteenth (Protestant Reformation). They were particularly critical of our trying still to live in the last century religiously with its methods and terminology. They noted that such phrases as "mourner's bench" and "praying through" came, not from Scripture, but directly from the American frontier. Though Graham is the most noted mass evangelist of our time, he said the "protracted meetings" also came from that earlier period in our history and are archaic and dated if Christians take seriously the personal challenge to witness and serve.

What can we do about the world which moves so fast? We can hide our head and hope the changes and surprises will disappear. Or we can challenge every new thing in the name of sacred tradition and work desperately to maintain the status quo. Or we can confront the new day with the new creation in Christ and imbue it with meaning and relevance. It is pretty clear that no group, including the church, can hold back history with its bare hands. Anyway, it is God's history, so why should we try?

We know from reading the pioneer D. S. Warner, his words and work, that he was a great innovator. He did not want to stop the world and get off. The question: Can we make the timeless gospel current, and be to our generation what ancient men were to theirs?

Reaching for the Moon

IS NOT MAN displaying an unholy curiosity in reaching for the moon? The space effort is costing us $7 billion this year; $23 billion since 1961. Critics call this "moon money" and say it would be far better spent on earth— on our cities, on poverty, on hunger, on education, on air pollution.

A deeper problem, though often an unspoken suspicion of Christians, is that the scientist is an enemy within the gates and the great destroyer of faith.

When our first hero, John Glenn, flew into space, my mind turned to Psalm 139:7: "Whither shall I go from thy Spirit? Or whither shall I flee from thy presence? If I ascend to heaven, thou art there!" I thought also of the noted scientist who began his classes, "Gentlemen, shall we again today think God's thoughts after him."

Many, though baffled, have spoken helpfully on this issue. "Man wants to know, and when he ceases to do so, he is no longer man" (Nansen). "Space is the modern equivalent of the American frontier" (Wheeler). "Space exploration is one of man's great adventures, and the U.S. must participate with brilliance and boldness" (Killian). "The new space science will enlarge our concept of God" (Dahlberg).

Science and religion are not enemies. They cannot be, for God's truth is one and total. Both deal, not with proofs, but with evidences. Both fall back on faith, the reality of the unseen. "The things that are seen are transient, but the things that are unseen are eternal" (2 Cor. 4:18). Both are nourished by reverence and worship: "Be still, and know that I am God! I will be exalted" (Ps. 46:10).

I am among those who believe God intends that man's explorations should not be limited to the earth, but should include all of his creation. The mountains and crators on the moon are no more sacred or out of bounds than the hills of Brown County, Indiana. We landed men there by 1970, as President Kennedy predicted. If I were young and brave enough, I would like to be with them as their chaplain. Instead and in the meantime we must work to understand and conquer human nature on planet Earth.

I refuse to run and hide with my faith when the discoveries of microscope and telescope are announced. They no longer shock and defeat. I welcome scientists into our churches. Many outdo us in faith.

The Week That Was

A YOUNG MINISTER announced that he would present a series of sermons in which he would figuratively hold *Time* magazine in one hand and the Bible in the other and attempt to relate the two sources. His concern was to apply the ancient instructions of the Christian faith to the ongoing human story, to permit early wisdom to inform him and his congregation about the week that was and the week to come. It proved to be quite an exercise, almost a game, for the young minister. The reactions of the people were mixed, mostly favorable. All were cautioned against one thing: the sin of irrelevance in the preaching and practice of religion.

What are some of the by-products of such an experiment in preaching? For one thing, the group dismissed false illusions concerning the gravity of the hour and the titanic problems confronting man. They saw not only change, but unprecedented speed of change. Man is born to conflict and will be eternally tested in the world. His religion will be tested—not in the sanctuary, but in society; not on Sunday, but the other six days.

Moreover, the gospel is being validated in the week that was. The gospel is the good news that "God was in Christ reconciling the world." How does *Time* magazine alert us? It indicates that social rottenness will weaken the gospel's witness, if left unopposed. Materialism and sensate culture will choke it out and make it barren. Racial discrimination will invalidate it. The magazine also brings lessons about the cosmos and man in it. Thermonuclear war will annihilate civilization if we do not have the wisdom to replace hatred with love and teach others to do so. The conquest of outer space will be futile if, in the process, we have failed to conquer inner space, that yawning chasm between what we are and what we ought to be.

Look at the other piece of literature, the Bible. There is utter realism about it, but it is also a book of hope. These dangerous days are not the final moments of civilization. The sky has not fallen. God is still in his heaven, even if all is not right with the world. I affirm that there is not a problem facing mankind today on which we would not receive wise counsel if we explored at depth the wisdom given us in the Word of God. The Bible is not a fragile document, but the sturdy account of quest and conquest, man's and God's.

Our task is to proclaim a relevant gospel in the week that was. Our challenge is to make the Christian faith livingly, situationally, dynamically captiviating.

INSTANT OATMEAL

WE HAVE just purchased our first box of instant oatmeal, but still have most of it in the cabinet. Take it from us, it isn't worth your money. Though I am not sure what a mixture of glue and sawdust might taste like, I think it might be like this.

95

Now, I have really been fooled on a lot of other instant things and should have known better. But, in spite of many unpleasant experiences on quickie cures, answers, and programs, I probably will be sucked in again.

Cautions against instantaneity cover almost all known categories. Think with me of the many golden promises held out in advertising, promotion, business, education, and even religion. Let's begin with the last. Where I come from in Kentucky, the credentials for the ministry, some thought, were a black book and a white shirt. Those were the days of instant ordination. Believe it or not, we are not as far past those days as some of us would like to believe. Whereas we would insist that a doctor, an attorney, an engineer, or an educator have maximum credentials, having followed patiently the rigors of his discipline, we probably can recall some premature ministries.

In the public sphere there are instant news, instant success and fame, instant vocations, instant riches, instant power. In the area of relationships there are instant friendships, instant marriage, instant static, instant divorce, instant adolescence, instant maturity. Strangely, in race relations many have expected instant Negroes.

In religion there are instant missions, instant evangelism, instant authority, instant laymen, instant emotions, instant answers. In fact, the temptation to the magic of oversimplification and speed is very great in religion. We probably feel that there is some logic to this, since the urgency of the gospel is massive. The "now" of our salvation is very commanding.

However, let us see again that "with the Lord one day is as a thousand years and a thousand years as one day" (2 Pet. 3:8). God apparently has infinitely more patience, program, and power than we have realized. It appears that temptations to shortcut are humanly, not divinely, initiated. Thus endeth the lesson of the oatmeal.

Beards and Sideburns

WE HAVE HAD a couple of young men in Seminary in recent months with attractive full beards. I have been reluctant to observe that they remind me of our picture of D. S. Warner—afraid they would shave them off. All of it has made me curious to compare hair styles between 1880 and 1970, and A.D. 50, for that matter. If we could get authentic pictures, they might look strangely similar. One minister said he didn't object to long hair if it were no longer than Jesus'. When asked how long that was, he guessed probably about the neck and ears. That gem of wisdom has not solved much, yet probably put that minister on pretty good terms with his son, which is not to be minimized.

Those with a little less nerve, both students and professors, are growing sideburns, in all sizes and shapes. These appear to be a matter of mild protest—something like boiling your draft card. What is the real point regarding the stormy changes of fashions. What do long hair and short skirts, wide ties, pink shirts, blunt shoes tell us about the great issues of freedom and faith, human cussedness and sainthood? Probably not as much as we earlier assumed.

Are we learning anything from fads and fashions? Yes. We are learning not to base our religion on them. They can change overnight. To be up to date may be to be out of date. Thankfully, we have gotten past the ascetic hangups, when bobbed hair, jewelry, cosmetics, neckties, were determinative of spirituality. The internals have become more crucial for us than the externals.

Jesus' words have come home to us: "Judge not, that you be not judged. For with the judgment you pronounce you will be judged, and the measure you give will be the measure you get" (Matt. 7:1-2). It is in bad taste for any of us to play God, given our own fallibility and indiscretions in fads. So, we are allowing great emancipation and individuality in our religious expressions. Does this not make for considerable risk? Yes, it does. We may have some freakish looking characters among us. But the opposite, religious rigidity and legalism, is insufferable. And who wants to be on the committee to check out beards and costumes?

Mrs. Billy Graham has been quoted as saying that she likes beards. If he came out with one, it could give the beard such apostolic sanction that it could last another five years, and that is really more than we can stand.

HOPE
Soundings in Hope

Hope

WE ARE BORN to hope, and the range of our hoping is both for this world and the world to come. For example, all of us hope for health and healing, but the ultimate of it will come beyond death, in the resurrection. E. Stanley Jones has said that healing may come in one or more of these ways: Medicine, surgery, scientific nutrition, climate, mental suggestion, direct action of the Spirit of God, and the resurrection. That last is not a neat escape from a physical and theological dilemma, but the conclusive statement of our faith. Certainty about the resurrection is at the heart of the Christian hope.

Some find it hard to accept the inevitability of death, but the shadow of it has been thrown across all our paths. No person escapes. Even in the midst of life we are dying, and the end is coming soon. Now look at our Lord's victory. "The truth is that Christ has been raised from the dead, as the guarantee that those who sleep in death will also be raised" (1 Cor. 15:20, TEV). This is the convincing sign of God's gracious provision for our future. The resurrection of Jesus removed the "sting of death."

The believer's hope is not a blind optimism, a faint expectation, a tame desire. The source and substance of it is the living God (1 Tim. 4:10). As Victor Hugo says, it is "the word which God has written on the brow of every man." The fulfillment of hope will be inaugurated by Christ's return (Titus 2:13). God will "clothe us" in a new body appropriate for our continuing life of fellowship with him. "In this hope we are saved" (Rom. 8:24).

But we do not wait until the end. "Character produces hope, and hope does not disappoint us" (Rom. 5:4-5). The present fruit of the Christian's hope is the unshakable confidence in the face of all adversity. Ask any pilgrim who has traveled through danger, disaster, and defeat. He is not hapless, helpless, hopeless; he is nerved to face life's challenges without flinching. He travels under the arching rainbow of hope.

The Defeat of Death

AGNES AND I PURCHASED our cemetery lots a few weeks ago. Now, don't ask me why we did it so soon or waited so long. And this announcement is no prompting for readers to go and do likewise.

I heard recently of a sermon titled "Friend Death." I did not hear the sermon, but find it hard to guess the complimentary words spoken in the light of Paul's observation that the last enemy is death (1 Cor. 15:26). Of course, it is possible that pain, old age, infirmity would make one's home-going quite welcome. In such a case, the welcome of death would surely be balanced by the high doctrine of the Christian hope of the resurrection.

What massive decisions should be made prior to death? The overarching one, of course, is to be ready always with the forgiveness of our sins. In addition to buying the burial lot, another good counsel is to make one's will. Add the great spiritual disciplines of worship, obedience, stewardship, witness, and service "until he comes."

How can one be practical and wise about dying and yet keep from being victimized by the sales propaganda of the mortician? How can one honor the physical body and yet resist the commercial and cultural pressure to beautify the corpse and paganize our memorial services?

Another question: How can the relatives, the physician, the pastor, in honesty and helpfulness, assist the saints in dying gloriously? How can they capture Vachel Lindsay's poetry mood of General William Booth entering heaven?

Paul, of course, helps us most in 1 Corinthians 15. Death, which is inevitable, is a means of deliverance. It is uniquely personal and, strangely, is conquered by actually dying. It is a summons from God, providing a gate and passage to the resurrection. This is the miracle we celebrate at Easter.

Paul tells us that the Christian is a new creation (2 Cor. 5:17). His confident expectation centers in Christ. With the risen Lord, he participates in the new being. Yes, death is real and death is final, but a new body, fit for the new world of the spirit, conquers and continues. Jesus both illustrates it and guarantees it, for he is the "first fruit of those who sleep."

All right, we'll take some kidding about our will and our new cemetery lots. The mood, however, about the defeat of death will not be fun, but joy and actualization. The Christian hope enables us to live with courage and die with dignity.

Resurrection: Faith and Miracle

"WINTER IS on my head, but eternal spring is in my heart," said Victor Hugo. It is the time of the year to celebrate life and hope and the miracle of resurrection.

Why do we say miracle? Because death is real and total and it will take God's miracle to reverse it. As James Angell wryly put it, "Remember that the ultimate death rate is still 100 percent. You would be getting gypped if everyone got to die and you didn't." In the biblical view man dies and literally ceases to exist. Death destroys totally the earthly form, the whole man (body and soul). There is nothing about man which goes on forever as a natural and automatic agent. Personality has no momentum of its own to carry it past the barrier of death. That is the last enemy (1 Cor. 15:26).

Greek philosophers misled us. They, not the Christians, taught that the soul is a free floating spirit which moves immortally in a future invisible world.

Now we approach the ultimate affirmation: At Christ's coming the dead are touched by the miracle of resurrection. It is God's act of new creation. Ours will be a "spiritual body," a new eternal form suited to the new world of the spirit (1 Cor. 15:35-54). It is a glorified flesh, no longer subject to temptation, sin, and death. But note. It is still a body, a person, still "you," recognizable as an individual with your own personal identity. And there we are together in all our individuality, concreteness, and particularity. Oh, the wonder of it all!

Wouldn't we like to have a lot of our questions answered? Such as, what are we and where are we in the interim? Apparently it is not given to us to know. We can do some guessing. The canons of time and space do not apply to the world to come. A thousand years is as a day with God. So we simply "wait" for the resurrection in God's good time. We go to sleep and "wake up" in the morning, not knowing (or worrying) that time has passed. We need not be concerned about missing it if our name is on the Lamb's Book of Life. If, before our physical death we are "risen with Christ," we can count on the same after it.

Did we say guessing? It is better than that. Though no one has returned from beyond, we have the example of our Lord. The body given Christ at his resurrection is the promise and proof of the victory we too shall have. Can we not take it by faith? Come to think of it, that is the way we accept all of God's bounties—by faith. The glory and joy of life with Christ is worth it all.

"Birth of God" Talk

DID YOU hear the Russian joke? Yuri Gagarin, the first cosmonaut, returned from his trip to report to his countrymen. He said to Khrushchev, "During the flight I looked carefully, and saw God out there." Khrushchev replied, "I knew it all the time, but don't tell anyone else." Later Gagarin reported to the Metropolitan of the Russian Orthodox Church, "During the flight I looked carefully, but failed to see God out there." The Metropolitan replied, "I knew it all the time, but don't tell anyone else."

Humor? Surely not a knee slapper. But the yarn is interesting commentary on the kind of God talk one may hear today. Such talk is not very clarifying or edifying. However, it should not have surprised and shocked us as it did. We Christians asked for it.

Talk about fuzzy thinking! We applied substance and physicality to God, and geography and plush materiality to heaven. We ought to know better than that for even man (much less God) is not basically and ultimately fleshly and physical, but spiritual.

I would have to say that these "death of God" days have been the most informing and soul stretching I have known. Like J. B. Phillips, I have felt that if you can't believe in God today, the chances are your God is too small. The announcement of the death of God threw many into an emotional tizzy, not to say panic. It pushed others back to ask seriously for the first time who God is and what he is up to today. Frankly, it contributed to the theological birth of God for many of us.

The Gospels and the epistles have two striking three-word definitions of God: "God is spirit" (John 4:24); "God is love" (1 John 4:8). These prompted Nels Ferre to call for a return to the language of the Bible, which he feels depicts God as "the creative spirit who is love."

The John 4 incident of Jesus with the woman at the well cautions us against assigning God to a spatial location. The living God does not dwell on mountaintops nor in temples. He is not "over there or up there or out there." The caution is clear: We must stop thinking of God as a concrete entity, a finite object among other finite objects.

God is Reality, with a capital R. He is the invisible, eternal Reality from whom all things come, in whom all creation lies, and to whom all finite spirits return. Now even that sentence fails. Words and definitions must partly misrepresent his Reality. Reason and logic are totally inadequate. We had better come to God in the mood of awe, reverence, worship, and trust.

The Keys to the Kingdom

TWO KEYS unlock the doors to the kingdom of God. They are repentance and faith. I love these words, for they tell me what I need to know about beginning and continuing the Christian life. Let them be on the lips of the missionary, the evangelist, the witnessing Christian, and he will be giving the best possible directions to the Kingdom. Let them guide his own life, and it will be pleasing to God. If we apply repentance and faith wisely, we will have boiled all the fat out of the recipe for righteousness.

When Jesus came into Galilee preaching, this was his theme. He said, "Repent ye, and believe the gospel" (Mark 1:15). These were the directions he gave Simon and Andrew, James and John, by the lakeside. They too were caught up in the message.

Repent! What do we mean? The word itself means to think again, to change one's mind. It says that we turn around, do an about-face. This is the manward side of salvation, though the promptings for it are from God. We recognize we are on the wrong road and open up to a radical reorientation of life and its relationships. To repent is to accept God's judgment upon us and to confess that in his sight we are sinners.

Faith! What do we mean? It speaks of our heartfelt trust and openness to God and his faithfulness (1 Thess. 5:24, 1 Cor. 1:9). It is not merely the assent of the intellect or the acceptance of propositions or doctrine, but the obedient response to Christ and the Word of God. It is a putting on of Christ and complete confidence in his forgiveness. It might be compared to the believability of our family doctor in whom I have such respect and trust that I put myself in his hands for his advice and medicine.

I will be tempted to add frills and extras to repentance and faith, but I had better not. They are biblical, experiential, dynamic, and permanent. I will come back to them again and again. They are important to holiness people. If I have not exercised something of penitence and faith today, I probably am not current in my Christian experience.

That the Fire May Burn

ON MAY 24, 1738, "about a quarter before nine" in the evening, John Wesley felt his heart "strangely warmed." He said further, "An assurance was given me that he had taken away my sins, even mine." At last Wesley found the certitude he had been yearning for.

Aldersgate is a good example of the experiential basis of conversion. When we come to Christ in repentance and faith, we are promised the new birth, the new creation. Transformation takes place at the deepest level of personality, namely the will. Again Wesley: "Saving faith is not barely a speculative, rational thing; a cold, lifeless assent; a train of ideas in the head; but also a disposition of the heart."

The inner heartwarming experience cannot be captured by propositions, confessions, or techniques. We do not need someone outside us prompting us and approving us in the faith. Our repentance will bring its own confirmation. The new life in Christ is self-validating. As Paul puts it in Romans 8:15-16, "You have received the spirit of sonship. When we cry, 'Abba! Father!' it is the Spirit himself bearing witness with our spirit that we are children of God."

Man's alienation from God is manifested in contemporary life by a number of significant symptoms. Most of us, for example, experienced guilt, hostility, and anxiety. These were present among us at various levels of strength and varieties of expression. We knew ourselves to be wrong in God's sight and we sought his forgiving word in Christ. In a redemptive confrontation we found a personal breakthrough into spiritual reality. We knew it and we testified to it.

In a sentence the ingredients of the new experience are somewhat as follows: individual regeneration, emotional warmth, personal godliness, and dedicated service. We are placed in the realm of grace. The spark of renewal has been struck and it will burn hotter and brighter in our pilgrimage of discipline and obedience. Faith enlarges into feeling.

There's a Word for It

WORDS ARE DOORS which open us up to meanings. If we can use the old words in new ways we should have better thoughts and ideas. Have you rejoiced, as I have, that the new Bible translations and paraphrases throw a bright light on familiar passages? The new words are illuminating. Let's try a few.

Faith means "openness to God." It says that God can be trusted and that we abide in his faithfulness (1 Thess. 5:24). A modern writer likes to say that faith is our acceptance of the truth that we have been accepted by God.

Grace means that "God is for us." Men are saved, not by what they own, or know, or do, but only by the unmerited favor and grace of God. Now we can put the first two words together: "By grace you have been saved through faith; and this is not your own doing, it is the gift of God" (Eph. 2:8).

Revelation means that "God is speaking." This is the only thirty-five cent word in the list, but it is very important. The speaking is in the present tense and is done through the Word, through the Spirit and the church, through nature and history. Yes, in many ways God is speaking, is conveying his meanings to us through revelation. Is anybody listening?

Love means "caring." It is that concern, that attention, I direct toward God and my fellowman. But even the impulse to love is planted by God. "We love because he first loved us" (1 John 4:19). As J. B. Phillips puts First Corinthians 13:6, "Love . . . is not touchy. It does not keep account of evil." Yes, love is caring, without reservation, without hesitation, without calculation.

Hope means that "the future is still open." This too is God's gift as man waits trustingly and courageously for the divine promptings. Hope gives buoyancy and patience for the rigors of the journey and a vision of the prize at the end of the race. It speaks of openings, not closings.

Words are keys to unlock doors to theology, to relationships, to life. "Open sesame!"

God's Symphony

IT WAS IN midwinter that I heard the Indianapolis Symphony Orchestra, but it spoke to me of God's symphony in the spring. Now spring is upon us.

The blend of horns, strings, percussions, under the baton of a gifted director, made beautiful music. There was harmony and purpose, wonder and hope, message and mystery in the musical experience.

Even in December, I thought of May and Babcock's:

Back of the loaf is the snowy flour,
  And back of the flour the mill,
And back of the mill is the wheat and the shower,
  And the sun, and the Father's will.

He who has eyes and ears, let him look around and let him listen in the spring. So much is breaking forth. "Earth's crammed with heaven, and every common bush afire with God."

I see gardens and flowers. Their fragrances and colors are a perfect example of God's symphony. The sparrows and bees, chirping and buzzing, seem to be enjoying it all and contributing their part to it.

I see the whispering pines and the rolling rivers, the fleecy clouds and the starry heavens, the sunrises and the sunsets. Yes, the earth, with a thousand voices, praises God and participates in his symphony. "The heavens are telling the glory of God; and the firmament proclaims his handiwork" (Ps. 19:1).

We are talking here about evidences for the existence of God from the natural world around us. They are very impressive, and especially so to those whose lives have been touched by God's forgiveness in Christ. God's symphony makes inspiring music, particularly if we are acquainted with the master musician.

God is creator; he made all things. He made man in his own image. The magnitude of creation, the precision of it, the harmony of it, the beauty of it!

God is sustainer and orderer; he is not at a distance looking on. He is in the midst of his world, still creating and involving himself in its destiny. The whole universe is charged with the grandeur of God.

How shall we keep in touch with the musician? It surely will not hurt to keep contact with the parts, the chords, even a scientific appraisal of all that God is up to. But these are not enough for some, and perhaps not the best beginning. The better way is to meet a Person in trust and commitment. Our faith then is our openness to God.

The Best and Worst of Times

RECALL THE WORDS of Charles Dickens as he began *Tale of Two Cities,* "It was the best of times; it was the worst of times." Many today feel that we indeed are confronting the best and the worst of times. It is a baffling mix. To put it another way, some of us may be pessimistic about our immediate problems but optimistic about the long run.

Our day is not that unusual really. Note another time when the best and worst were mixed: the year 1809. In that year Napoleon was running roughshod over Europe, and people were waiting with bated breath for the latest news of the war. As it turned out, the decisive factors that year were not the battles but the babies. A whole host of heroes crept into the world. In 1809 authors Alfred Lord Tennyson was born in England and Oliver Wendell Holmes and Edgar Allen Poe were born in America; William Gladstone, statesman, in England, Louis Braille, teacher of the blind, in France, and Felix Mendelsohn, composer, in Germany; in America recall 1809 as the birth of Cyrus McCormick, inventor, in Virginia, and Kit Carson, frontier scout, and Abraham Lincoln, president, in Kentucky. What a year: Napoleon and Lincoln! In the worst of times God sends a decisive baby into the world. In the "fulness of time," (Herod in Palestine and Augustus Caesar in Rome) God sent his Son (Gal. 4:4).

History has its ups and downs, its periods of speed and slowness, creativity and bafflement. Many feel that these are particularly bad times and can cite striking evidence to prove it. Then they become prophets of doom. I personally am not willing to settle for this. Could it possibly be God's acceptable time, his day of salvation (2 Cor. 6:2)? This decade may both test us and tell us.

As the prophetic Spirit is active in the church and in the world, it can only be apprehended by persons of vision and faith, and it can only be accomplished by persons of commitment and courage. These are our acceptable gifts to God in the best and worst of times.